CliffsNotes™

All Quiet on the Western Front

By S

IN THIS BOOK

- Learn about the Life and Background of the Author
- Preview an Introduction to the Novel
- Explore themes, character development, and recurring images in the Critical Commentaries
- Examine in-depth Character Analyses
- Acquire an understanding of the novel with Critical Essays
- Reinforce what you learn with CliffsNotes Review
- Find additional information to further your study in CliffsNotes Resource Center and online at www.cliffsnotes.com

WILEY

Wiley Publishing, Inc.

About the Author
Susan Van Kirk holds a B.A. from Knox College and an M.Ed. from the University of Illinois. She has taught English for 30 years in Monmouth, Illinois.

Publisher's Acknowledgments
Editorial
Project Editor: Elizabeth Netedu Kuball
Acquisitions Editor: Gregory W. Tubach
Glossary Editors: The editors and staff at Webster's New World™ Dictionaries
Editorial Administrator: Michelle Hacker

Production
Indexer: York Production Services, Inc.
Proofreader: York Production Services, Inc.
Wiley Indianapolis Composition Services

CliffsNotes™ *All Quiet on the Western Front*

Published by:
Wiley Publishing, Inc.
909 Third Avenue
New York, NY 10022
www.wiley.com

Copyright © 2001 Wiley Publishing, Inc., New York, New York
Library of Congress Control Number: 00-107806
ISBN: 0-7645-8671-8
Printed in the United States of America
10 9 8 7 6 5
1O/RT/QT/QT/IN
Published by Wiley Publishing, Inc., New York, NY
Published simultaneously in Canada

For general information on our other products and services or to obtain technical support, please contact our Customer Care Department within the U.S. at 800-762-2974, outside the U.S. at 317-572-3993, or fax 317-572-4002.

Wiley also publishes its books in a variety of electronic formats. Some content that appears in print may not be available in electronic books.

Table of Contents

How to Use This Book

CliffsNotes *All Quiet on the Western Front* supplements the original work, giving you background information about the author, an introduction to the novel, a graphical character map, critical commentaries, expanded glossaries, and a comprehensive index. CliffsNotes Review tests your comprehension of the original text and reinforces learning with questions and answers, practice projects, and more. For further information on Erich Maria Remarque and *All Quiet on the Western Front*, check out the CliffsNotes Resource Center.

CliffsNotes provides the following icons to highlight essential elements of particular interest:

Reveals the underlying themes in the work.

Helps you to more easily relate to or discover the depth of a character.

Uncovers elements such as setting, atmosphere, mystery, passion, violence, irony, symbolism, tragedy, foreshadowing, and satire.

Enables you to appreciate the nuances of words and phrases.

Don't Miss Our Web Site

Discover classic literature as well as modern-day treasures by visiting the CliffsNotes Web site at www.cliffsnotes.com. You'll find interactive tools that are fun and informative, links to interesting Web sites, and additional resources to help you continue your learning.

At www.cliffsnotes.com, you can obtain a quick download of a CliffsNotes title, purchase a title in print form, browse our catalog, or view samples such as a table of contents or a character map quickly and easily. See you at www.cliffsnotes.com!

LIFE AND BACKGROUND OF THE AUTHOR

To the biographer and student of literature, Erich Maria Remarque, who has been called the "recording angel of the Great War," was an enigma, a man rife with contradictions and contrasts. He admired stylish women, Impressionist art, an antique Lancia convertible and a racy Bugatti, and Chinese art from the Tang dynasty and was obsessed with pacifism, free speech, and privacy. Following the overnight success of his landmark war protest novel, *All Quiet on the Western Front*, Remarque was able to indulge numerous sensualistic tastes and escape the mundane hometown that he so vividly describes in his prose. Expunging his middle name—Paul—and replacing it with Maria, his mother's name, he immortalized the name Paul in Paul Bäumer, the speaker of his novel, who lives out the neorealistic horrors of trench warfare—chlorine gas, bayonets, tanks, flamethrowers, mangled messenger dogs and horses, hunger, dysentery, lice, longing, confusion, and despair.

A member in good standing of Gertrude Stein's "lost generation," Remarque, in life and literature, witnessed the cataclysm of the two world wars. Like Hemingway, with whom he is frequently compared, Remarque centers on the fighting soldier, the victim who bears the horror of war's uncivil onslaught. Characterizing his contemporaries as "hard . . . afraid of feelings, without trust in anything but the sky, trees, the earth, bread, tobacco that never played false to any man," he attempted to exorcise his own postwar trauma by re-creating on paper the amorphous hell of the western front, where his high school graduating class was thrust from pubescent patriotism into callous cynicism before completing their second decade.

Early Years

Born Erich Paul Remark (he later changed his name out of embarrassment over a novel he published in 1920), the novelist was the son of bookbinder and master machinist Peter Franz Remark and his wife, Anna Maria Stallknecht Remark, both descendants of devout French Catholic expatriates to the Rhineland following the French Revolution. He was born June 22, 1898, in Osnabrück, Westphalia, a prosperous industrial town in northwestern Germany, twenty-five miles from the Netherlands. As members of the hard-pressed lower end of the working class, the Remarks shuffled almost annually among a series of quarters between 1898 and 1912, once residing in rooms above Prelle, the publishing company where his father was employed.

A bookish lad known affectionately as Schmieren, or "Smudge," to his contemporaries, Remarque was the third child of a family of four. His older sister Erna was followed by Theodor Arthur in 1896, who died at the age of five. In 1903, Elfriede, his ill-fated baby sister, completed the family. The Remark children, brought up in a strict Catholic household, attended the local Präparande, a parochial school where Erich often got into scrapes with school authorities, particularly Professor Konschorek, whom he later skewered in the seriocomic character Kantorek. To pay for school books, fish for his aquarium, and a few boyhood niceties, Remarque, a talented pianist and organist, gave piano lessons to young girls who often seemed more drawn to his Aryan good looks than to his pedagogy. When time allowed, he collected butterflies, stones, and stamps, joined a gymnastics club, fished for sticklebacks in the Poggenbach River, performed magic tricks, and composed poems and essays.

Except for school teaching, few professional choices lay ahead for men of Remarque's social class. Accepting necessity, he entered elementary education courses at the Lehrerseminar in 1913. In 1915, he and several other idealists formed a literary brotherhood around mentor Fritz Hörstemeier. The following year, his essay about young cadets, "From the Time of Youth," a poem titled "I and You," and a short story, "The Lady with the Golden Eyes," were printed in the Osnabruck newspaper.

The Great War

On November 26, 1916, shortly after winning thirty marks in an essay contest, Remarque was drafted as a musketeer, or infantryman, and completed basic training at Osnabrück's Westerberg Camp. He then was transferred to Celle, from which he visited his mother, hospitalized for cancer, which ended her life on September 9, 1917.

Earlier that June, as a "sapper," or lineman in an engineering unit, Remarque had begun building bunkers, pillboxes, and dugouts behind the Arras Front, east of the Houthulst Forest and south of Handzaeme, frequently working at night to avoid sniper fire.

On July 15, 1917, Remarque's company advanced to Flanders for some of the most savage fighting of World War I. Trench warfare dispelled his youthful idealism, particularly after he carried his buddy Troske out of enemy fire and Troske died like the fictional character Kat. He was treated for minor shrapnel injuries and later died of a head wound from a shrapnel splinter while he was being carried to a medic.

During five months of heavy rain, the Allied and German armies hammered away at each other, gaining little ground; in four months, the two armies chalked up 770,000 casualties, many of them non-combatants. Spattered with grenade splinters in his neck, left knee, and right wrist, Remarque exited the fray on July 31, evacuated by troop train from the aid station in Thourout to St. Vincenz Hospital, Duisburg, outside Essen. A competent, respected soldier, Remarque was treated well and worked briefly as an orderly room clerk. On his off hours, he dated an officer's daughter, began writing his first novel, and set the poems of Ludwig Bäte to music. Rejoining the 78th Infantry in October, he was declared fit for duty only four days before the armistice.

Postwar Life

After mustering out on a medical discharge in 1918, Remarque suffered postwar trauma and disillusionment, complicated by regret that his wounds ended his hopes for a career as a concert pianist, and by grief over his mother's death. For a time, he posed illegally as a much-decorated first lieutenant, accompanied by Wolf, his shepherd dog. Occasionally, Remarque dressed extravagantly and wore a monocle. For the next ten years, he would cast about for a life's work, but for now he settled into a special veteran's seminary, where he chaired a student association that rebelled against the practice of treating war veterans like teenagers.

With average grades, Remarque graduated on June 25, 1919, having specialized in Goethe's verse and Herder's folk songs. During this year he wrote three poems—"C Sharp Minor," "Nocturne," and "Parting"; three sketches, "Ingeborg: An Awakening," "Beautiful Stranger," and "Hour of Release"; and two essays, "Nature and Art" and "Lilacs." He also received his first assignment as a substitute teacher from August 1 to March 31, 1920, in Löhne, where he boarded with a local family. Once again the Osnabruck newspaper published a poem of Remarque's titled "Evening Poem." He also published a novel that he would later regret called *The Dream-Den*. It described Remarque's prewar literary circle and was so sentimental that the embarrassed author requested that his publisher, Ullstein, buy up all unsold copies. Following a month's unemployment, Remarque accepted a second substitute post from May 4 to July 31, 1920, in Klein-Berssen, where he lived in the teacherage. On August 20, he accepted a post in Nahne; however, he soon became bored and disgruntled with schools and resigned permanently on November 20.

Making do with minor jobs, including playing the organ at the Michaelis Chapel (a mental institution), selling fabric, writing art reviews for *Die Schönheit,* and carving tombstones for Vogt Brothers, Remarque moved to Hannover in October 1922 to work for Continental Rubber as a test driver and as an editor and writer of humor and verse for the in-house magazine, *Echo Continental.* Part of his responsibilities included travel throughout Europe as far south as Turkey. During this era, Remarque evolved his pseudonym, replacing his middle name, Paul, with Maria. Partly to distance himself from his sophomoric first novel, *The Dream-Den,* published in 1920, he adopted the spelling of his last name used by his great-grandfather, Johannes Adam Remarque. Three years later he published a poem, "To a Woman." In 1925, Remarque got his first break in writing as reporter and assistant editor for *Sport im Bild* (Sports in Pictures). His snobbish, stilted stories, including instructions for mixing cocktails, caused German critics to view these early writings as proof that Remarque was not serious about his art. Eager for social prominence, Remarque paid Baron von Buchwald to adopt him so that he might add a noble lineage, crest, and calling card to his résumé.

That same year, on October 14, Remarque married twenty-four-year-old dancer and actress Jutta Ilse Ingeborg Ellen "Jeanne" Zambona, an attractive, fashionable woman of Italian-Danish descent. Drawn to local social events, he developed a reputation for an upscale lifestyle. In 1927, he serialized a trivial car lover's novel, *Station on the Horizon*, in the company magazine.

Career as a Writer and Filmmaker

During this same era, concealing postwar trauma beneath public shows of wit and elitism, Remarque began confronting wartime torments, which he had incubated for a decade in his thoughts and dreams.

Within five weeks, Remarque, keeping alert on strong coffee and cigars, composed *Im Westen nichts Neues* (literally, *In the West Nothing New*), which was serialized in the magazine *Vossische Zeitung* from November 10 to December 9, 1928, then appeared in novel form the next year in English as *All Quiet on the Western Front*. Although publishers were skeptical that the postwar reader was still interested in World War I, Remarque's pacifist bestseller sold a million and a half copies that same year and in time was translated into twenty-nine languages. His countrymen, who bought most of the first printing, raised a confusing barrage of enthusiasm and criticism, stating that Remarque simultaneously dramatized pacifism by overstating wartime dangers, enriched himself by glamorizing the German battlefield, and promoted communism. The German Officers League, on hearing talk of a Nobel Prize nomination for Remarque, challenged the Swedish committee's wisdom in considering the proposal. The strongest voices against Remarque belonged to the National Socialist party, an ultranationalist group, who accused him of deliberately creating an antihero to denigrate war and of degrading Germany by victimizing manufacturers and medical staff as incompetent and opportunistic. Refusing his critics the satisfaction of verbal confrontation, Remarque rejected interviews, labeling his work nonpolitical so as to allow readers to draw their own conclusions. However, Remarque had touched a nerve, and the themes and ideas of this first best-seller would echo through his writing for the rest of his life.

The next decade brought further turmoil to Remarque's life. Long a seeker of affluence, he bought a Lancia convertible and dressed the part of the bon vivant. In 1930, he ended his formal marriage to Jeanne; the two remained together, however, and moved to Casa Remarque in Porto Ronco, on Switzerland's Lake Maggiore.

It was during this year that Remarque made his first move toward cinema with Universal Studio's black-and-white version of *All Quiet*, which used a 930-acre ranch in Irvine, California, for its battlefield setting. Starring Slim Summerville, 2,000 extras, and unknown actor Lew Ayres as Bäumer, the film, featuring real howitzers, land mines, and flamethrowers, received Academy Awards for best picture and for direction. In addition, scriptwriters Del Andrews, Maxwell Anderson, and George Abbott, as well as photographer Arthur Edeson, who melodramatically concludes with a close-up of Paul's hand clutching at a butterfly when he is hit by a sniper's bullet, also received Academy Awards. Labeled by critics as an American landmark and a major coup for Universal, the film was touted by the National Board of Review and named picture of the year by *Photoplay*. *Variety* magazine commented that the League of Nations should "buy up the master-print, reproduce it in every language to be shown to every nation every year until the word *war* is taken out of the dictionaries." The movie reached vast audiences and caused the growing Nazi party great concern. In the early 1930s, Hitler youth, prodded by propagandist Goebbels, rattled German movie audiences by overrunning theatres, releasing white mice, and tossing beer bottles and stink bombs. Within weeks, the movie was banned.

Undeterred, in 1931, Remarque published *The Road Back*, a study of postwar trauma. Similar in tone and theme to Hemingway's *The Sun Also Rises*, the novel delineates the slow recovery process, which finally reawakens young survivors to nature and healing. But war was to continue haunting Remarque. Because he was a sincere patriot, Remarque was unable to shut out Germany's attempts to kindle another world war. Immersed in antique Egyptian artifacts, Venetian mirrors, music, and priceless paintings by Cezanne, Daumier, Picasso, Degas, Toulouse-Lautrec, Matisse, Pissarro, Renoir, and van Gogh, Remarque tried to ignore the hatred of Hitler's propagandist, Josef Goebbels, who plotted to punish the author for antiwar sentiments. Goebbels cranked out a stream of lies and innuendo, linking Remarque with bohemians, Jews, and communists. He also charged him with removing money illegally from the country, concealing Jewish ancestry, championing internationalism and Marxism, and besmirching the memory of heroes killed at Ypres, in Flanders, and in France. In 1933, zealots burned Remarque in effigy in the Obernplatz, the ornate plaza facing Berlin's opera house. That same year, in the company of books by Thomas Mann, Ernest Hemingway, James Joyce, Maxim Gorki, Bertolt Brecht, and Albert Einstein, *All Quiet on the Western Front* was reduced to ashes in front of the Berlin Opera House. Ironically, Soviet Russia repeated the ban later in 1949.

Despite the reaction of the book burners, *Three Comrades*, a sequel to *All Quiet* extolling the virtues of battlefield friendships, was published in 1931. This pre-World War II novel showed a glimpse of Remarque's love for Jeanne Zambona and moved beyond male bonding to a sweet, but doomed, romantic interest. In January 1938, to spare Jeanne the loss of her Swiss visa and a forced return to Germany, Remarque married her a second time and negotiated an open relationship, giving each of them the freedom they desired. In June, Remarque was stripped of his German citizenship. Throughout his life, he remained sensitive to his nationality, proclaiming, "I had to leave Germany because my life was threatened. I was neither a Jew nor orientated towards the left politically. I was the same then as I am today: a militant pacifist." Later, he moved farther south, settling in Paris and Antibes with longtime companion Marlene Dietrich, cultivating a coterie of expatriates, and drinking heavily. Publicity about Remarque's lifestyle on the French Riviera boosted sales of his books. In response to growing anti-Nazi sentiment, the 1930 film of *All Quiet* was reissued in the United States in 1939. Padded with voice-overs, prologue, and epilogue, this version proved less emphatic than the original. Shown the world over, it did not appear in Remarque's homeland until 1952, when it was shown in Berlin.

Movies would continue to spread Remarque's pacifism. Two films were made of Remarque's novels in 1937 and 1938. First, Universal Studios filmed *The Road Back*, starring John King, Richard Cromwell, Slim Summerville, Andy Devine, Spring Byington, and Noah Beery. The film so inflamed the German embassy that the director was forced to minimize Remarque's anti-Fascist themes. The following year, MGM released Joseph L. Mankiewicz's version of *Three Comrades*, using a screenplay by F. Scott Fitzgerald and starring Robert Taylor, Robert Young, Franchot Tone, and Margaret Sullavan, whose performance received an Oscar nomination. Reviews from *Time* and the National Board of Review remarked on the film's beauty, skillful actors, and sensitive direction.

Life in America

A new life and citizenship awaited Remarque in America. Shortly before Hitler precipitated war by invading Poland, Remarque, too proud to accept proffered German citizenship, escaped the Gestapo by traveling the back roads through France, sailed on a Panamanian passport aboard the *Queen Mary*, and entered New York as a literary star. To reporters, Remarque predicted World War II and looked to President Franklin Roosevelt as the world's only hope. In 1941, he published *Flotsam* (entitled "Love Thy Neighbor" in German), in a serialized version in *Collier's*. It featured the sufferings of exiles fleeing Hitler's Germany. Remarque collected material for the work from numerous poignant stories that were standard fare among his many expatriate friends. The same year it appeared with a new name as United Artists' *So Ends Our Night*, but it was unsuccessful as a movie and received only one Academy Award nomination, for Louis Gruenberg's music. The film starred Fredric March, Frances Dee, Glenn Ford, Margaret Sullavan, and Erich von Stroheim.

Remarque's time in Los Angeles was followed by a celebrated social life on the east coast. While working for various movie studios, Remarque lived in a colony of German expatriates in west Los Angeles until 1942, when he moved to New York's Ambassador Hotel and eventually to an apartment on East 57th Street, which he considered his permanent home. A lover of beauty, Remarque squired starlets to the Stork Club, Ciro's, and 21, making friends with Greta Garbo, Charlie Chaplin, Cole Porter, F. Scott Fitzgerald, and Ernest Hemingway. He felt at home with the style and companionship of the "glittering people." However, even at this safe distance from Hitler's menace,

Remarque was not spared the beheading of his sister, fashion designer Elfriede Scholz, in a Berlin prison. The Nazis' perverted insult to her grisly demise was a bill for ninety marks sent by the executioner to Remarque, the brother whose pacifism had precipitated their unstinting spite.

The next few years would bring more books and films but also great sadness. When the war ended, Remarque published *Arch of Triumph* (1945), a major novel that depicted the struggles of pre-World War II exiles and was set in Remarque's beloved Paris. The novel highlighted the stoic, existential strength of Ravic, one of his most memorable protagonists. Later, in 1952, he would revisit his sister Elfriede's death in dedicating his next novel to her, a victim of Nazi vengeance. *Spark of Life*, describing concentration camps, was the first of Remarque's works to remain unfilmed. In the author's description, he wrote ". . . if it is a good book it will be widely read and through it, some people who did not understand before may be made to understand what the Nazis were like and what they did and what their kind will try to do again." During the years between these two novels, Remarque saw two more of his books made into film, the recently published *Arch of Triumph* and *The Other Love*. The latter was a 1947 movie about a melodramatic failed romance starring David Niven and Barbara Stanwyck. In 1948, Lewis Milestone again directed a Remarque title when *Arch of Triumph* was brought to the screen by United Artists. Starring Charles Boyer, Ingrid Bergman, Louis Calhern, and Charles Laughton, the teary pre-World War II reflection lost three and a half million dollars. However, like *All Quiet*, it would later be revived for television.

Life became less oppressive for Remarque in his last two decades. In 1954, he published *A Time to Love and a Time to Die*, dedicated to his close friend, and later his wife, Paulette Goddard Remarque. This novel achieved popular success as a Book-of-the-Month Club selection. Its focus, the effect of Gestapo tactics on civilians, bares the scars inflicted by Germans who chose complicity with the Nazis as a means of coping. The abridged German version of this novel incurred controversy because the editors excised the full horrors of Remarque's incisive view of the Nazi perversion of the national soul. In 1955, Remarque scripted Michael Musmanno's *Ten Days to Die* under the title *The Last Act*, which was filmed by an Austrian company to depict Hitler's final days. An effective vehicle, it starred Oskar Werner and earned appreciative comment at the Edinburgh Film Festival. A second Remarque book-to-film, *The Black Obelisk*, quickly followed in 1956, and its setting returned to hometown scenes following World War I. It contains more ribaldry and humor than Remarque generally incorporated in his writing. That same year, *The Last Station*, Remarque's only play, was performed under the title *Berlin 1945* at Berlin's Renaissance Theatre during a cultural festival. A reenactment of the Russian takeover of Berlin, the play pitted two conquering armies against the greater good of democracy and free speech, one of Remarque's more heartfelt issues. It would be revived in America two decades later.

An American citizen since 1947, Remarque sought an amicable divorce from Jeanne in Juarez, Mexico, in 1957. On February 25, 1958, he married actress Paulette Goddard. A trim, vibrant, virile man, Remarque enjoyed peace and contentment in his final marriage, which appeared to be a match of true love. A reader of Malraux, Proust, Flaubert, Balzac, Stendhal, Poe, Schopenhauer, Nietzsche, Rilke, London, Wilder, and Zen philosophy, he also devoted himself to book discussions, long walks, and collecting Iranian rugs and Chinese bronze figurines, which his wife later sold to relieve the burden of guarding his costly treasures.

Later Years

During the 1960s, Remarque expanded the short story "Beyond" into a novel, which he titled *Heaven Has No Favorites* (1961). It described a star-crossed love story between a young sanitarium patient and a race car driver. The following year, he wrote *Night in Lisbon*, which centered around the theme of stateless emigrants and captured the rootlessness of many of his compatriots.

Remarque and his work remained close to the film industry during the 1960s. During his entire life he wrote, scripted, and/or acted in ten films and was nicknamed the "King of Hollywood." In 1964, he consulted with other eyewitness experts for *The Longest Day*, a special effects extravaganza that won an Academy Award for Photography. The last work filmed in his lifetime was United Artists' *A Time to Love and a Time to Die*, which was four years in the making. Filmed in 1968, it brought together a youthful John Gavin and Swiss starlet Lilo Pulver, plus Keenan Wynn, Don Defore, Jock Mahoney, and Remarque, who wrote part of the dialogue and played Professor Pohlmann, earning worthy reviews for his acting skills. The movie, although frequently compared to *All Quiet* and to Hemingway's successful *The Sun Also Rises*, failed to meet critical expectations.

Few days remained for Remarque. Goddard remained at his side through rehabilitative respites from arthritis, stroke, and congestive heart failure, until his death from an aortic aneurysm in St. Agnese Hospital, Locarno, Switzerland, on September 25, 1970. She respected his wishes to be buried privately near Lake Maggiore, in the land that had become his home when Germany rejected him, and never disclosed to the public his private papers and journals.

However, two works were published posthumously and Remarque's novels continued to be filmed or revived in various forms. In 1972, *Shadows in Paradise* replayed his familiar theme of postwar trauma for exiled Europeans. The following year, Leonard Nimoy and Swedish actress Bibi Andersson starred in Peter Stone's English adaptation of *The Last Station*, titling it *Full Circle*. It riveted audiences in New York and Washington, D.C. Five years later Warner Brothers tackled *Heaven Has No Favorites*, renaming it *Bobby Deerfield*. Although directed and produced by Sydney Pollack and starring Al Pacino as the Grand Prix racer opposite Marthe Keller as his dying love interest, the film was a flawed effort.

In 1979, *All Quiet* was revived a third time, this time as a TV movie starring Richard Thomas as Paul, Ernest Borgnine as Kat, Ian Holm as Himmelstoss, and Patricia Neal as Paul's mother. Filmed in Czechoslovakia, it utilized Tarrazin, a World War II concentration camp, as the barracks. The final scene depicts Bäumer as killed in action while observing a lark. Several years later, a second version of *Arch of Triumph* was reshot for television in France in 1985, following an abortive attempt in 1980. Unlike the original, in this version the chemistry of Anthony Hopkins and Lesley-Anne Down resulted in a more successful re-creation of Remarque's novel.

Throughout his lifetime, Remarque revisited the themes and ideas of his earlier amazing landmark antiwar novel, *All Quiet on the Western Front*. In both novel and film form, his ideas continued to cause great consternation and anger to oppressive governments and kept in the public eye the tremendous sacrifice, death, horror, and destruction caused by war.

INTRODUCTION TO THE NOVEL

Introduction

When Erich Maria Remarque was mustered out of the Great War in 1918 on a medical discharge, he returned home to a life devoid of hope and changed forever. His earlier dreams had included becoming a concert pianist, but, because of war wounds, that ambition was no longer a possibility. During the time he had been in combat, his mother had died and now he had time to mourn and regret. Remarque, like many of his lost generation, suffered postwar trauma and disillusionment. This one huge and overwhelming event in his life—World War I—would haunt him forever and influence practically everything he would write. Again and again, Remarque would return to scenes of the war and to postwar Germany for subjects of his novels. The world would read his words and understand the questions of his generation, and the critics would treat his book kindly. Modern readers return again and again to his words because their powerful message delineates a dehumanization vastly surpassed by modern technological warfare.

An interview from the state archives in Osnabruck gives the reader some understanding of Remarque's reasons for writing *All Quiet on the Western Front*. The author states:

> It was through . . . deliberate acts of self-analysis that I found my way back to my war experiences. I could observe a similar phenomenon in many of my friends and acquaintances. The shadow of war hung over us, especially when we tried to shut our minds to it. The very day this thought struck me, I put pen to paper, without much in the way of prior thought.

Modern medicine knows more about post-traumatic stress disorder, but in Remarque's day it was unchartered water. His point of view—similar to the common soldier of any nation—provides the reader with insights concerning the shocking events that led to the alienation and displacement of his entire age-group. Remarque's words brought swift reactions in postwar Germany and positive responses from critics.

Although the German government—especially the Third Reich—banned and often burned Remarque's book because it dared to criticize the government and militarism, western critics were largely positive about his novel. Their words predating World War II—a time when military leaders were optimistically predicting the end to international aggression—addressed the poignance of the World War I German soldier's naivete and vulnerability, particularly during the aftermath, when the massive destruction of innocence produced a generation of drifting, traumatized men. Whether the survivors were German or American, British, Russian, or French, their post-traumatic stress could be seen across cultures and languages. Later criticism of Remarque after World War II dealt with the realism, existential alienation, and war profiteering outlined by Remarque's novel.

Despite Remarque's words and the millions of readers who have read his novel through the years, the modern era has seen great cataclysms that redefine the inhumanity of war with technological innovations that Remarque's generation could never have imagined. World War II, the Korean War, Vietnam, the Israeli Seven-Day War, Russia's attack on Afghanistan, the Persian Gulf War— all were fought with even more terrible weapons, including the atomic bomb, biological exterminators such as anthrax and nerve gas, and computerized missiles capable of sniffing out targets with little or no danger to the programmer. Instead of the hand-to-hand combat and the trench warfare of the past, today's modern wars can kill millions at the push of a button. More than ever, Remarque's characterization of war as a dehumanizer has much to say against this backdrop of a civilization creating efficient and impersonally fired weapons of mass destruction.

A Brief Synopsis

The record of several schoolmates who represent a generation destroyed by the dehumanization of World War I's trench warfare, *All Quiet on the Western Front* tells of their enlistment in the army at the urging of their teacher, Kantorek, whose wisdom they trusted. Paul Bäumer, a sensitive teenager, serves as central intelligence, the prototypical young infantryman whose youth is snatched away by the brutality of war.

Behind German front lines between Langemark and Bixschoote in 1916, only eighty of the original one hundred fifty soldiers of the Second Company remain fit for duty. Paul and his comrades have acquired a bit of battle experience, including the loss of Joseph Behm, the first of their group to die. Franz Kemmerich, his leg amputated, faces imminent death. A letter from Kantorek calling them "Iron Youth" stirs Kropp's anger.

The soldiers, recalling Platoon 9's brutal basic training in Klosterberg, abandon their idealism as a result of the sadistic tutelage of Corporal Himmelstoss. In its place, they evolve a strong comradeship, which bolsters and protects them far better than the now useless information they learned in school. Franz Kemmerich, Paul's friend, dies after the amputation of his leg. Müller inherits Kemmerich's boots.

Kat, the shrewd, self-reliant scrounger, manages to supply his friends with beans and beef. Paul and the others, excited by news of Himmelstoss' arrival at the front, recall the night before they left the training camp, when they trapped their drill instructor in a bedspread and beat him.

Paul's unit, which includes some inexperienced recruits, lays wire at the front. As they wait for return transportation, a bombardment and poisonous gas barrage pin them in a cemetery, churning up corpses from old graves. At dawn, a truck returns the men to their billets.

Himmelstoss arrives and tries to ingratiate himself with his former drill students. The men ignore and abuse him. Himmelstoss succeeds in having Tjaden and Kropp punished for insubordination. Kat and Paul thwart a guard dog and steal a goose, which they roast and share with the others.

Second Company spends the summer near the front, fighting savagely with grenades, bayonets, and sharpened shovels. The thirty-two men who survive return to the rear in the fall to rest.

The company moves farther behind the lines than usual, where they eat, sleep, and spend time with willing French girls, whom they shower with gifts of food. Paul returns home for a seventeen-day leave. Alienated by battle trauma, he lacks ambition and is unable to enjoy the pleasures of his youth. He despairs at his mother's weakness but enjoys the humor of Mittelstaedt tormenting Kantorek, now a member of the home guard and a poor specimen of a soldier.

Paul receives additional training at a camp on the moors, where he observes the sufferings of Russian prisoners of war, who must barter and scavenge garbage in order to stave off hunger. He thinks of them as pathetic human beings rather than adversaries and wishes that he could know them better.

Back with his unit, Paul feels more at home with comrades than he did with family. Inspected by the Kaiser, Second Company returns to the front. While on patrol, Paul becomes separated from the others and fatally wounds Gérard Duval, a French soldier, in self-defense. Face to face with a dying enemy, Paul is remorseful and tries to ease the man's sufferings. Returned to the dugout with his comrades, he confesses to the killing, then calms himself by concluding that "war is war."

Paul's luck changes when he is assigned to the supply depot and enjoys food and comfortable beds. While evacuating a village, Paul and Kropp are shot and sent by train to St. Vincenz Hospital. Kropp's leg is amputated. Paul recovers and goes on leave, but sorry to leave his friend behind, he returns to front-line duty.

In the summer of 1918, the war goes badly for Germany. Even rations, which are adulterated with unwholesome additives, are in short supply. Troops suffer dysentery and nervous exhaustion from the seemingly endless assaults of the Allies. Paul is the last remaining member of his schoolmates. He carries Kat to an aid station to be treated for a shin wound. On the way, Kat is hit in the head by a tiny splinter of shrapnel and dies. Paul collapses.

In October 1918, Paul, recently returned from two weeks' leave to recover from poisonous gas, is killed on a quiet day, shortly before armistice ends the war.

List of Characters

Paul Bäumer (BOY-muhr)   The sensitive twenty-year-old narrator of the novel, who has written poems and a play entitled "Saul." Paul reaches manhood during three years' service as a soldier in the Second Company of the German army during World War I. His loss of innocence during the cataclysm is the focus of the author's antiwar sentiment.

Tjaden (JAH-duhn)   A thin, nineteen-year-old soldier with an immense appetite. A former locksmith, Tjaden is unable to control his urine during sleep and draws ridicule from Himmelstoss. Tjaden's drive for revenge reveals the negative side of an otherwise peaceable personality.

Müller (MEW-luhr)   A scholarly young man who continues studying his physics books and thinking of exams. Pragmatic to a fault, he inherits Kemmerich's soft airman's boots, then wills them to Paul as Müller lies dying with an agonizing stomach wound.

Stanislaus "Kat" Katczinsky (STAN-ihs-laws kuh-ZIHN-skee)   About forty years old, Kat, a crusty, jocular cobbler and veteran of the battlefield, serves as a noncommissioned tutor and father figure to Paul and the others, who depend on him for locating food, arranging for light duties, and helping them cope with the exigencies of survival, such as listening for incoming shells and sensing an attack. Not the least of his skills is the ability to joke in order to take the men's minds off bombardment.

Albert Kropp (kruhp) The best student in Paul's class, he joins Paul in rebelling against Himmelstoss' bullying. Albert is promoted to lance corporal, then threatens suicide after his leg is amputated at thigh level. Taking comfort from his companions, he resigns himself to an artificial limb.

Leer (lair) Paul's mature schoolmate and math whiz who titillates his comrades with details of sexual intercourse, which the others have yet to experience. In the summer of 1918, Leer bleeds to death from a hip wound.

Franz Kemmerich (frahnz KEHM-muh-rihk) Paul's slim childhood friend and fellow volunteer who longs to be a forester. In bed 26 at St. Joseph's, his rapid decline and death from a leg amputation is Paul's first eyewitness experience with personal loss.

Haie Westhus (HY-ee VEHST-hoos) A nineteen-year-old peat digger, Haie prefers a military career to a lifetime of manual labor but dies of a back wound, never to achieve his ambition to be a village policeman.

Detering (DEE-tuh-rihng) An Oldenburg peasant who hates to hear horses bellowing from pain and is plagued by worries about his wife, who must tend their farm alone. Filled with longing for home, when cherry trees are in bloom, he deserts. After his capture, he is sent before a field tribunal and never heard from again.

Kantorek (KAHN-tow-rihk) The hometown schoolmaster, a chauvinistic sloganeer, who fills his students' heads with impassioned speeches about duty to the Fatherland and sends them letters that depict them as "Iron Youth." As a member of the local reserves, he is tormented by his former student Mittelstaedt, who teams him with the school janitor to demonstrate how poor a soldier Kantorek turns out to be.

Corporal Himmelstoss (HIHM-muhl-shtahs) A former postman and wartime drill instructor caught up in an illusion of power. Himmelstoss demonstrates bullying and tyranny, incurring wrath for humiliating two bed-wetters. At the front, Himmelstoss proves a sorry soldier, requiring Paul's prodding to keep him from cowering in the trenches during an attack. After the company cook goes on leave, Himmelstoss assumes the post and redeems himself by rescuing Haie.

Joseph Behm (YO-suhf baym) A chubby teenager who hesitates to volunteer for the army, then joins three months before he would have been drafted. Blinded on the battlefield, Joseph wanders helplessly into the line of fire and becomes the first of his classmates to die.

Lieutenant Bertink (BAYR-tihnk) Commander of the Second Company, Bertink sets a worthy example for his men, whose respect he earns. He doles out light punishment for Tjaden and Kropp and demonstrates heroism by knocking out an advancing flamethrower.

Kindervater (KIHN-duhr-VAH-tuhr) Himmelstoss forces him, a bed-wetter, to share a bed with Tjaden, also a bed-wetter. Ironically, his name means "child father."

Ginger Second Company's red-haired cook who worries that he has cooked enough rations for one hundred fifty men when only eighty remain; he cares more about conserving food than about the number of fallen soldiers.

Tiejen (TEE-juhn) A soldier who calls for his mother and holds off a doctor with a dagger, then falls dead.

Sergeant Oellrich (UHRL-rihk) A sniper who takes pride in the accuracy of his shooting.

Heinrich Bredemeyer (HYN-rihk BRAY-duh-MY-r) A soldier who informs Paul's mother about front-line dangers.

Mittelstaedt (MIHT-tuhl-shteht) Paul's friend who commands the home guard and uses his authority to humiliate Kantorek, their former schoolmaster, even parroting some of Kantorek's favorite sneers. To circumvent punishment, Mittelstaedt relies on his ongoing relationship with the daughter of his superior officer.

Boettcher (BETT-chuhr) A spruce, proud soldier, he was formerly a porter, a staff employee, at Paul's school. Boettcher shares with Kantorek the job of pushing a barrow to fetch bread.

Josef Hamacher (YO-suhf HAH-mah-kuhr) An inmate at the Catholic hospital who shares a ward with Albert, Paul, and Peter, Hamacher has a "shooting license" because he is considered brain damaged and shares inside information about the Dead Room.

Chief Surgeon A staff member at the Catholic hospital, he delights in experimental operations on the flat feet of soldiers, whom he ruins for life.

Little Peter An undersized, curly-haired ward mate suffering a severe lung wound. He resists being taken to the "Dead Room," then amazes his buddies by becoming the first patient to return.

Franz Wächter (frahnz VEHK-tuhr) A ward mate, he suffers an arm wound that hemorrhages during the night. Failing rapidly, Franz is taken to the Dead Room and never returns.

Sister Libertine A nun at the Catholic hospital, she cheerfully assists Paul and Albert and jubilantly wheels Peter back from the Dead Room.

Berger (BAYR-guhr) The most powerful soldier in the Second Company. During the summer of 1918, he commits an error in judgment and is wounded while trying to rescue a messenger dog under fire.

Gérard Duval (zhuh-RAHRD doo-VAHL) A French soldier, a typesetter in civilian life, he is knifed to death by Paul. Seized with guilt for killing him, Paul searches Duval's wallet for an address and discovers letters and pictures of Duval's wife and child.

Johann Lewandowski (YOH-hahn LAY-vahn-DOW-skee)
A forty-year-old Polish veteran, he has occupied a ward in the Catholic hospital for ten months while recovering from an abdominal wound. His wardmates keep watch while he makes love with his wife, Marja, whom he hasn't seen for two years.

Kemmerich's Mother
A hometown friend of the Bäumer family, Franz's mother humiliates her son by following him to the station and imploring Paul to watch over her son. Later, unable to bear the thought of Franz suffering at length, she forces Paul to take a strong oath that the report of her son's instant death is the truth.

Paul's Mother
A long-suffering, self-sacrificing woman with recurrent cancer, Paul's mother scrimps to provide him with potato-cakes, whortleberry jam, and warm woolen underpants. During his last night at home on his first furlough, she sits late by his bedside to express her concern for his welfare. Later, she receives treatment at a charity ward in Luisa Hospital.

Paul's Sister
Scarcely described in the text, Paul's sister greets him at the door when he returns on leave and helps him tie his tie when he dresses in civilian clothes. Together, Paul and his sister wait in line for meat scraps, but come home empty-handed.

Paul's Father
Sharing a strained relationship with his son, Paul's father accompanies his son to the local tavern and later visits him at the camp on the moors before Paul returns to the front.

Three French Girls
Occupants of a house across the canal from Paul's billet, the girls, unable to buy food, welcome soldiers who pay their way with army rations. The brunette, Paul's pick of the three, proves more interested in food than in the men who supply it.

Kaiser
The authority figure who leads Germany during the Great War and whom Paul's friends perceive as the cause of the war.

Character Map

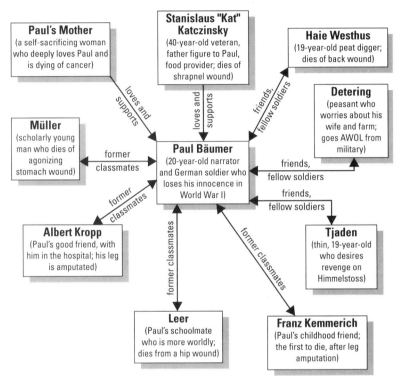

CRITICAL COMMENTARIES

Remarque prefaces his novel with a disarmingly simple two-sentence statement of purpose, which clarifies that his book neither accuses nor confesses, nor is it meant to be an adventure story. The author explains that he is merely trying to characterize his generation, the young men who fought the Great War and who were destroyed by it. The task Remarque sets for himself suggests the heavy personal burden that consumed his private thoughts for a decade following his own departure from the western front.

Having endured shelling, poisonous gas, and poor-quality medical treatment in the field, Remarque was admirably suited for the role of spokesperson for a generation of young people who, whatever their level of involvement, loss, or outlook, were fated to shoulder guilt, remorse, trauma, and dysfunction. Through loss of ideals and beliefs held sacred by prewar society, survivors, unmoored from the safe anchorage usually accorded the young, drifted into despair, disgust, and spiritual unrest. Deprived of innocence by nightmarish sounds and sights that they were incapable of articulating to family and friends, they survived on the edge, never quite in tune with the present and hopelessly detached from the future. They were, as Gertrude Stein commented to a war-maimed Ernest Hemingway, a "lost generation."

Chapter One

Summary

Five miles behind the front lines between Langemark and Bixschoote, Paul Bäumer's company is at rest. They have had very little sleep for the fourteen days since they relieved the front line and seventy of their one hundred and fifty men are dead at the hands of Russian gunfire. The cook, Ginger, has fixed rations for the one hundred and fifty and, after arguing with the lieutenant, grudgingly consents to give all the food to the eighty soldiers left, including double rations of smokes. As the narrator remarks, "Today is wonderfully good."

The narrator is Paul Bäumer, a nineteen-year-old boy who is already battle-hardened in this first chapter. As they rest, Paul describes the group of German schoolboys who enlisted with him at the prodding of their schoolmaster, Kantorek. One by one he introduces the doomed group as Albert Kropp, "the clearest thinker"; Müller, who carried books and "dreams of examinations"; and Leer, bearded and a frequenter of officers' brothels. These young men were in Paul's school class, and the novel follows their lives. Along with these comrades, Paul describes several others who will become part of his wartime company: Tjaden, a nineteen-year-old locksmith, skinny but a big eater; Haie Westhus, nineteen, a peat digger with huge hands; and Detering, a peace-loving peasant with his wife and farm always on his mind. In contrast to these youngsters is a forty-year-old veteran named Stanislaus Katczinsky or "Kat." He is "shrewd, cunning, and hard-bitten" with "a remarkable nose for dirty weather, good food, and soft jobs." A cobbler in civilian life, he is older than the boys and assumes the role of leader and he seems to have a special bond of friendship with Paul.

While the company is resting, they play cards, read letters and newspapers, and smoke. Realizing how lucky they are for this respite, they do not discuss the war. Instead, Paul reflects on their differences from the new recruits; using the common latrine as an example, he cites their own lack of embarrassment and hints of their war-driven knowledge of "things far worse." Clearly, the main focus of soldiers is their stomachs and intestines.

The mail catches up with the company and there is a letter from Kantorek, their former schoolmaster, who encouraged them to join the war effort with his tales of glory. Bitterly, Paul speculates, "There were thousands of Kantoreks, all of whom were convinced that they were acting for the best—in a way that cost them nothing." Paul considers one story in particular of Joseph Behm, who was not meant for combat but was persuaded to join. Shot in the eye and left for dead, he crawled around No Man's Land until he was shot again and killed. Thinking of the fragile Behm, Paul reflects on how their young, innocent world was destroyed at the first bombardment.

The scene shifts to the aid station, where Paul, Kropp, and Müller visit their buddy, Franz Kemmerich. Insensible to the amputation of his injured leg, Kemmerich puts on a cheerful face, yet fails to hide a serious physical decline. This visit is the first of many they will make to hospitals or dressing stations where Paul smells carbolic, pus, and sweat. Paul realizes immediately that Kemmerich will die, because he is used to seeing death now in a man's face and eyes. Paul bribes the attendant to give Kemmerich more morphine while Müller callously tries to persuade their friend to let him have his English boots of soft, yellow leather. The boys know the orderlies will steal the boots when Kemmerich dies. Kemmerich doesn't want to give up the boots, so they remain with him for now. But the school friends leave, foreseeing this first death among their group.

Back at the camp, Paul realizes he must write a letter to Kemmerich's mother at home. Meanwhile, Kropp is angry because Kantorek has called them "Iron Youth" in his letter. Reflecting on this phrase, Paul thinks, "Youth! We are none of us more than twenty years old. But young? Youth? That is long ago. We are old folk." This transition has already happened prior to Chapter One; the ex-schoolboy can already see and accept death on the face of his friend.

Commentary

The first chapter of *All Quiet on the Western Front* sets the tone quietly for the violent and often gruesome story to follow. Remarque takes us away from the action long enough to introduce the characters and setting, produce the initial tone of the narrator, set in motion various themes to be illustrated shockingly, and string together a group of symbols that will be amplified.

The characters and setting are introduced through the eyes of the novel's narrator. Paul's comrades are partly school chums who spent many years together reading books, studying, and listening to their teachers. Paul ponders on Müller, with his textbooks of science and mathematics. Where will those textbooks take Müller in this war? Then there is Kropp, the quiet, thoughtful boy; these personal characteristics are hardly good ones for a hardened soldier. And Behm certainly represents the slaughter of the innocent, already lost to impractical dreams. Paul thinks about the girls and the dances that might have been. In fact, when Paul goes home later, he realizes these memories are from another time and another world. Germany, outmanned and outpaced by better-supplied Allied forces, struggles to hold on to slender gains, purchased at the price of thousands of dead and wounded men.

Remarque also elaborates in this chapter on the tone of the narrator, Paul Bäumer, speaking for his creator. Paul seems at first philosophical and uncaring. Through his narration, we will see benchmarks in the soldiers' progression from innocence to a realization of the cruelty and inhumanity of war. Already Paul describes the abundance of food as a mere "miscalculation" instead of commenting on the extent of the company's deaths. His discussion of the public latrine and his concern for creature comforts rather than people seems already to make us aware of his progress in this downward spiral. But we also see a touch of humanity when he goes to visit Kemmerich with the others. He is being practical about the boots and the theft in the hospital, but he also sees death in his friend's eyes where a few months ago he did not even know the specter of death. He bribes the attendant to give Kemmerich extra morphine to ease his suffering.

Theme

A number of themes, which will be abundantly developed throughout the novel, begin in this introductory chapter. Again and again Paul mentions his generation's loss of innocence. "Youth? That is long ago. We are old folk." He comments on Detering, who thinks of his farm and wife, an example of the peace-loving peasant swept up in a place and time from which he cannot escape. Loss of innocence is paralleled by the tragic loss of traditional values and faith. Kantorek, the object of Paul's bitterness, is only one of many German role models who convinced the lost generation that it was their duty to go to war. As Paul remarks, "The first bombardment showed us our mistake, and under it the world as they had taught it to us broke in pieces." Their lost innocence is partly a result of the violence and cruelty of man against man. They come up with euphemisms such as "pushing up daisies" to describe the massive death they see all around them. Before his story is over, Paul will end up running from one trench to another like a cornered animal. Even in this first chapter, he describes vividly the knowledge that the "old hands" like himself know compared to the raw recruits.

Callousness and greed are also a part of this story. We see this in the soldiers' casual attitude toward eighty deaths, the cook's reluctance to part with any extra morsel for the remaining soldiers, Müller's desire for Kemmerich's boots while his heart still beats, the theft of Kemmerich's watch, and the bribery of the greedy orderly.

In contrast to these themes, Remarque also provides contrasting motifs of warmth. There is comradeship and rare humanity on the part of the lieutenant who champions his men, the shared fears and terrors, the communal deprivation and loss, Paul's pretense with Kemmerich that he is not dying, and his friendship with Kat. Another positive theme is Remarque's insistence that, through all of the mud, the gore, the deaths, the starvation and disease, the aesthetic pleasures of nature, in the form of flowers, butterflies, trees, and meadows, continue all around, as though the people and their violence do not matter.

Literary Device

Nature emerges as a symbolic value in this story with red poppies blooming amid latrine boxes, white butterflies fluttering around and floating on "the soft wind of late summer," and a flowery meadow blooming on as part of the natural order of things despite man's war. Whenever Paul begins to bow down under the terrible burden of his eyes, he momentarily finds peace in the world of nature. Its innocence is a welcome refuge from the grim horrors of war.

The boots of Kemmerich are another symbol; they already had belonged to an English airman. Then they became Kemmerich's and, because he is dying, they may soon become Müller's. Each time the boots change hands they are worn as long as the owner lives and become a somber reminder of the fragility of life. These bright spots in so dismal an introductory chapter are dampened by Paul's realization of his past: "And we saw that there was nothing of their world left. We were all at once terribly alone; and alone we must see it through."

Glossary

(Here and in the following chapters, difficult words and phrases, as well as allusions and historical references, are explained.)

haricot beans   any of various edible beans, especially kidney beans.

quids   pieces of chewing tobacco.

English heavies   cannons, or field artillery.

dressing-station   a first-aid tent where wounded men are stabilized before being transported to military hospitals.

pushing up daisies   [Slang] dead and buried.

dust-up   [Slang] a commotion, quarrel, or fight.

dixie   an oversized iron cooking pot.

non-com   [Informal] a noncommissioned officer; an enlisted person of any of various grades in the armed forces.

quartermaster   an officer whose duty it is to provide troops with quarters, clothing, equipment, and so on.

billets the quarters or lodging provided for military personnel.

observation-balloons   the enemy's method of locating the dugouts of soldiers and assaulting them with grenades and light firearms.

anti-aircraft shells   explosive projectiles fired at enemy aircraft.

misere ouverte   an open discussion of hardship.

nap   short for napoleon, a card game similar to euchre.

blighty   a wound that assures the victim a permanent departure from action.

No Man's Land   the unoccupied region separating opposing armies.

carbolic   a solution used as an antiseptic, disinfectant, etc.

morphia   morphine, a bitter, white or colorless, crystalline narcotic alkaloid derived from opium and used in medicine to relieve pain.

Chapter Two

Summary

Detached from home and the normal ambitions and concerns of a man of twenty, Paul ponders a play and some verse he left in his desk and realizes that his generation has "become a waste land." He thinks about Müller's pragmatic request for the boots, which Kemmerich will obviously never need again. Paul recalls how his group of twenty classmates, their plans for the future still in the formative stages, enlisted with the district commandant. After three weeks of basic training, their caustic victimizing by their drill instructor, Himmelstoss, deflates any romance the military ever held for them. Under Himmelstoss, they tolerate demeaning harassment, such as remaking beds, sweeping snow, softening stiff boot leather, performing guard duty on consecutive Sundays, and crawling on their bellies in mud. Paul and Albert, who usually bear the brunt of Himmelstoss' ill humor, challenge his power by dumping excrement on his legs. The act breaks his tyrannical hold over them, yet Paul explains that basic training suits the needs of a soldier by strengthening brotherhood and rendering them "hard, suspicious, pitiless, vicious, tough. . . ."

Returning to Kemmerich's bedside, Paul tries to boost his friend's morale. Having discovered the amputation of his leg, Kemmerich fears that he will die without achieving his ambition to become a head-forester. Paul, who observes Kemmerich's childlike nature, regrets his friend's impending death and vainly tries to encourage Kemmerich to return to Klosterberg for convalescence. An hour later, as Kemmerich begins to gasp, Paul begs an overworked surgeon for help, and then returns with an orderly to find his friend dead. Paul collects Kemmerich's belongings, unties his identification tag, and delivers the boots to Müller. They conclude the evening with sausage, hot tea, and rum.

Commentary

Theme

Chapter 2 provides a study in contrasts. On the one hand, Paul describes eloquently his "lost generation," and, on the other hand, he explains the hardening regimen that not only causes them to lose their innocence but also prepares them to survive at the front. The poignant scene with Kemmerich at the end of the chapter is a surviving indication of faith in man's humanity.

Paul continues to describe how "Our early life is cut off from the moment we came here, and that without our lifting a hand." He compares his comrades to the older generation who have already lived their middle age with homes, wives, families, and vocations. Paul and his peers have hardly even begun and, "in some strange and melancholy way we have become a waste land." Their heads were filled with romance and ideals, and they would never survive at the front with that education alone.

Unfortunately for Paul and his friends, fate intervenes in the person of Colonel Himmelstoss. Although the sadistic officer puts them through their well-described paces, he also teaches them more about survival in ten weeks than they ever learned in ten years of school. In their practical and chaotic world at the front, "a bright button is weightier than four volumes of Schopenhauer." So much for the schoolbooks; they learn to fight back in more subtle ways and become "hard, suspicious, pitiless, vicious, tough." This hardening regimen may seem cruel and senseless, but it prepares them for life at the front. The introduction of Himmelstoss is also important because he will later cross their paths in a very different way.

Theme

In the strange manner that life has of providing light out of darkness, Paul's battle with Himmelstoss elicits a value that Remarque continues to show throughout the novel. The brighter side of warfare is the comradeship that often develops in death-defying situations. As Paul says, a far more important lesson of their struggle is that "it awakened in us a strong, practical sense of *esprit de corps*, which in the field developed into the finest thing that arose out of the war—comradeship."

Character Insight

The poignant scene with Kemmerich in the hospital expands on the theme of companionship and evokes a faith in man's ability to care for his fellow man. Both men face reality, Kemmerich handing over his boots and Paul realizing that Kemmerich has only a few hours left. Paul nostalgically reflects on his childhood memories of Kemmerich, comparing him to a child even now. Unable to let his friend die alone, Paul cradles him in his arms and watches him silently cry as his life leaves him. But not one to wallow in self-pity, Remarque effectively undercuts this touching picture with the overworked and harsh doctor, who says he has amputated five legs that day and presided over sixteen deaths, and with the orderly who demands Kemmerich's bed immediately. The brutal picture of Franz hauled out on a waterproof sheet slices through the sadness of his last minutes. Paul collects Kemmerich's belongings, unties his identification tag, and delivers his boots to Müller. A moment of human kindness has been replaced with the cold, raw reality of death in war.

Glossary

"Saul"   a play whose title suggests the first king of Israel. In I Samuel 31:3–13 through II Samuel 1:1–27, David discovers Saul's body alongside that of the prince, Jonathan, and mourns their wretched deaths on the battlefield.

Plato to Goethe   Plato (427?–347? B.C.) was a Greek philosopher and Goethe (1749–1832) a German poet and dramatist; the passage indicates the education Paul and his peers had, covering everything from ancient Greek philosophy to the height of German Romanticism.

Frisian   people of Friesland or the Frisian Islands, near the eastern German-Dutch border.

parade-ground soldiering   ceremonial formation in dress uniforms.

esprit de corps   group spirit; sense of pride, honor, etc. shared by those in the same group or undertaking.

stickle-backs   small, bony fishes with two to eleven sharp spines in front of the dorsal fin.

saveloy   a highly seasoned, dried English sausage.

Chapter Three

Summary

After Second Company is reduced by nearly half, replacement troops arrive, seeming much younger than Paul and his friends. The replacements are actually only two years younger, but their lack of experience makes the age difference seem greater. Kat, the master scrounger, invites the newcomers to share beans, which he garnered in a trade with Ginger for three pieces of parachute silk. Later, Kat finds two loaves of bread, horse meat, a frying pan, salt, and fat. When they need a softer place to sleep than wire netting, Kat finds straw. As planes continue to drop explosives and battle for air superiority, Paul, who is quartered in a factory, sits below and observes the sky battle dispassionately.

Paul ponders how insignificant men like Corporal Himmelstoss, a former mail carrier, develop into bullies who abuse their authority with such meaningless games as "Change at Löhne," during which he forces men of lower rank to crawl under bunks. Keeping soldiers busy seems to be important so they won't have time to think or complain. The four friends recall how they plotted their revenge on Himmelstoss before they left for the front. Tjaden and Kindervater, whom the drill instructor humiliated for bed-wetting, have especially fond memories of their revenge. Following their former tormentor along a road from a pub on a dark night, the four soldiers joyfully wrapped Himmelstoss in a bedspread and, with Haie leading the attack, beat him mercilessly with kicks and punches and a whip, smothering his outcries with a pillow. Himmelstoss crawled away, and a veteran, impressed by the spirited young soldiers, proclaimed them "young heroes." Paul comments very simply, "We had become successful students of [his] method."

Commentary

In counterpoint to the death scene in Chapter Two, Kat's jolly opportunism lightens the mood of the men and the novel. In this chapter, Paul also reflects on how war changes insignificant men. He is joined in his musings by the others, who complain and vent their frustrations over how they would change things if they were in charge of the war.

Their commiserating leads to reminiscing about the night they joined in a lightning attack on Himmelstoss. The whole mood of the chapter is lighthearted, but it will be followed by a much darker account of life at the front.

Character Insight

Kat, although the veteran of the group, is not like the officers they describe. Kat explains to the raw recruits that they must barter tobacco or cigars when a scrounger like himself finds them food. He patiently listens to the plight of his friends and finds what they need. Besides the cold beans and beef, he finds straw, two loaves of bread, a frying pan, salt, and fat before the chapter is over. A pragmatist, Kat cannot understand why they need to practice an hour's saluting because Tjaden violated military protocol. Kat's sardonic philosophy is that if they are losing the war, it will be because they can salute too well.

In the meantime. there is an air fight going on above them and Paul is dispassionately watching it. No one seems particularly concerned with the fighting. The talk turns to postal carriers and why they turn into Himmelstosses when they get a little power. As Kropp notes about rise in rank, "As sure as they get a stripe or a star they become different men, just as though they'd swallowed concrete." Kat concurs, noting that military life brings out the worst in men, particularly the abuse of power over lesser men.

Literary Device

As they muse about the state of the war and particularly their officers, the men think back to the time they whipped Himmelstoss. They especially wanted to vent their rage over his inhumane treatment of Tjaden and Kindervater; joining ranks and illustrating their camaraderie, they unite against a common enemy. They will consider what they will have in store for their old nemesis after he joins them at the front.

Glossary

mess-tin   the compactly arranged metal plates and eating utensils carried by a soldier for use in the field; sometimes also referred to as mess kit or mess gear.

Prussians   people of a historical region of northern Germany, on the Baltic. The Prussian ruling class was regarded as harsh in discipline, militaristic, arrogant, etc.

bog-myrtle   a scented evergreen that produces black berries useful as a flavoring for stew.

bathing drawers   loose swimming trunks.

98 rifle   an upgraded Mauser rifle, which was safer and easier to use than earlier models. Adopted by the German military command in 1898, it had a 29-inch barrel and a five-round magazine.

Löhne   a city in the western part of Germany.

piss-a-bed   [Slang] a person who is unable to control urination, particularly during sleep.

regiments   military units consisting of two or more battalions and forming a basic element of a division.

garrison   a fortified place with troops, guns, etc.; military post or station.

reinforcement-depot   a central receiving headquarters where supplies are delivered for distribution to the field.

black-pudding   a hearty sausage made of blood, suet, and spicy, pungent flavorings.

old buffer   [Slang] old fellow.

Chapter Four

Summary

At nine o'clock in the evening, under cover of darkness, Paul's company, tense with the understood danger of their mission, boards trucks to travel down a bumpy road to lay wire near the front. Although they keep up a steady flow of repartee with a marching munitions column, Paul's group is disconcerted by a change in the usual pattern of British artillery, which begins firing before ten o'clock, an hour too soon. As they pass one particular house, Paul hears geese and glances significantly at Kat, who is already thinking about geese for dinner. As they near the front line they see the guns camouflaged and they smell the air, acrid with smoke. The fumes of powder can be tasted and the guns make the earth quake.

The young recruits are agitated but the veterans like Paul and Kat are thick-skinned and use the moment to teach the novices. Kat can recognize the type and size of the shells by the sounds, and he teaches the young recruits these differences. Meanwhile, Paul is thinking about the awareness of the front known to all soldiers; their senses are alert and they are changed from a relaxed state by "a tense waiting, a watching, a heightening alertness, a strange sharpening of the senses." As he ponders this, the lorries leave to collect them again at dawn.

While the night is lit up by the bombardment, Paul's detail goes about its task, pushing in iron stakes and stringing barbed wire at regular intervals. They finish long before the lorries return. Even though he is cold, Paul falls asleep for a while but awakens with a jolt. Kat calms him and ominously predicts a barrage. As incoming artillery begins, soldiers cry out and run for cover. Paul tries to console a young recruit, holding him in his arms as the rookie cries and shakes. It is a nightmare: Between explosions, cries of the wounded soldiers are heard and these are joined by the screaming of wounded horses. Detering is angered by the plight of the horses, but Kat explains that the other soldiers must help the men first. Not to be stopped, Detering aims his gun to shoot the distant horses, but Kat stops him before he shoots another soldier by mistake. Then they hear the horses being shot and Detering is upset that horses are used at all in war.

At three o'clock the next morning, the lorries return and Kat continues to be nervous about an attack. Not surprisingly, he is right, and the attack comes quickly and crushingly. There is no escape, and the men seek shelter. Paul catches a splinter in his arm and almost faints. He crawls into a hole and, realizing that they are in a cemetery, hides under a coffin. Kat, Kropp, and the young recruit are there also. As they shrink in terror at the barrage, Kat also realizes that gas is being used and warns them to put on their gas masks. The gas hovers and sinks into holes, forcing them to get above ground once again. However, another barrage begins and they are under attack with nowhere to hide.

A coffin hits the fourth man and Kropp keeps him from tearing off his gas mask. The injured man is the young recruit Paul comforted earlier, and they try to free his arm from underneath a coffin. As these anxious moments go on, Paul feels as though he is suffocating, because he is breathing the same air over and over in his gas mask. The cemetery is a mess of corpses and coffins. The barrage lets up and they discover that the recruit is hit on the hip; Kat surmises that he will never walk again and sees that the young victim's arm is bleeding also. As with the horses, Kat suggests they shoot the young recruit and put him out of his misery, because Kat knows what the young man will go through in his final days if they don't. Paul agrees, but before they can shoot him other soldiers arrive, so they must get a stretcher and call for a medic.

In the battle, five are killed and eight are wounded. Two of the dead lie in graves, so they simply throw dirt on them. An hour later, they reach the lorries and, in the desperate early morning hours, rain begins to fall.

Commentary

Theme

This chapter, one of the most dramatic in the book, depicts how Paul reacts to the intense fighting along the western front. As Remarque's most pointed explanation of how war reduces combatants to simple survival skills, the section contains reminders that humanitarianism and compassion quickly return, impelling the men to help the wounded and dying and to commiserate with maimed horses. Like animals themselves, the men cling to the earth in shell holes, trenches, and dugouts, foreshadowing their own burials, as well as the cemetery battle scene. As Paul notes, if fate proves false, the earth will receive them forever.

The consciousness of the front and its terrors streams through this chapter in Paul's thoughts. He says "there is suddenly in our veins, in our hands, in our eyes a tense waiting, a watching, a heightening alertness, a strange sharpening of the senses." This new consciousness is compared to the instincts of animals in fight-or-flight mode. All are changed from the relatively carefree soldiers they were in Chapter Three, or even from the stillness and peace of the ride in the lorries they experienced just moments ago.

Like a machine, the men become mere cogs in the wheel of war. They are part of a greater drama in which they are mere bodies. Even as they drive to the front, Paul himself feels sucked into this nightmare. He feels the front is "a mysterious whirlpool. Though I am in still water far away from its centre, I feel the whirl of the vortex sucking me slowly, irresistibly, inescapably into itself."

Man's inhumanity is stressed throughout this surreal nightmare. The screaming horses are like nature itself crying out at the actions of mankind. Euthanasia seems a fitting end for the horses as well as for the young recruit, whose life is shattered like his hip and arm. Both horse and man are but numbers in a huge battle that knows neither identities nor names. As Kat remarks that the young recruit is such "an innocent," Remarque seems to be commenting on the entire "lost generation" of this war.

Nature is also a key actor in this chapter. The earth becomes spiritually connected to mankind, "ashes to ashes, dust to dust." It is a refuge from the shelling, a site of horrifying death from gas, and a final resting place for literally thousands of nameless bodies that once were boys with names. Paul's description is an invocation to earth's refuge from the annihilation of man: "Earth with thy folds, and hollows, and holes, into which a man may fling himself and crouch down. In the spasm of terror, under the hailing of annihilation, in the bellowing death of the explosions, O Earth, thou grantest us the great resisting surge of new-won life." And even as nature shelters mankind, it also cleans up after him. When the battle is over, the rain comes to wash away the blood and the tears. As Paul says, "It falls on our heads and on the heads of the dead up in the line, on the body of the little recruit with the wound that is so much too big for his hip; it falls on Kemmerich's grave; it falls in our hearts."

Glossary

wiring fatigue the tedious task of laying barbed wire to slow an enemy assault.

lorries [British] motor trucks.

munition-columns narrow lines of soldiers accompanying artillery to the front.

Feast of the Tabernacles Sukkot; a Jewish festival celebrating the fall harvest and commemorating the desert wandering of the Israelites during the Exodus; observed from the 15th to the 22d day of Tishri, the first month of the Jewish year.

second sight the hypothesized ability to see things not physically present or to foretell events; clairvoyance.

Flanders to the Vosges from a region in northwest Europe, on the North Sea, including a part of northwest France and the provinces of East Flanders and West Flanders in Belgium to a mountain range in northeast France, west of the Rhine.

pioneer dump a supply source for the pioneers; here, a supply source for the infantrymen who are preparing the road for marching columns.

coal-boxes low velocity German shells; nicknamed "the black Maria," because they emitted dark smoke.

fete festival, entertainment.

nose-cap the metal tip of an explosive device.

gun-shy easily frightened at the firing of a gun.

Chapter Five

Summary

Following the desperate events at the front, Chapter Five creates a quiet mood of camaraderie among the group and especially between Paul and Kat. As the chapter opens, Tjaden rigs up a lid from a boot-polish tin, a wire, and a candle in order to kill lice. While they are relaxing, the group discusses a rumor that Himmelstoss has arrived at the front, transferred because he was too hard on recruits. Tjaden ponders his revenge.

In quiet moments, they discuss what they would do if peace occurred. Kropp says he would get drunk; Kat would go home to his wife and children; and Westhus would find a woman and a bed and then become a soldier with the Prussians, reasoning that, as a soldier, he would at least have food, a bed, clean underwear, clothes, and pubs in the evening. Tjaden ponders what he will do to Himmelstoss, and Detering worries about the harvest.

Himmelstoss arrives and he and Tjaden have an insult contest, with Himmelstoss demanding respect and Tjaden insulting him and eventually mooning him. As a result, Himmelstoss storms out, threatening a court-martial and Tjaden laughs so hard he dislocates his jaw, causing Kropp to hit him in order to realign it. They wonder if Himmelstoss will report Tjaden, who laughs that he could sit out the war in prison. The confrontation ends in the Orderly Room where Lt. Bertink gives Tjaden and Kropp a fair hearing and the bed-wetting incident is recounted. Tjaden gets three days open arrest behind a barbed wire fence, and Kropp gets one day. This is a light sentence; the others are able to visit the prisoners and play cards with them.

Chapter Five also includes a scene of friendship and affection between Paul and Kat. They go after a goose and end up killing, roasting, and eating it in a shed away from the others. It is a quiet moment of contentment, in which Paul declares to himself, "We are brothers." They take some of the meat to share with Tjaden and Kropp. As the chapter ends, Paul considers the contrast between their evening and the events of the war: "We are two men, two minute sparks of life; outside is the night and the circle of death." Then he sleeps.

Commentary

In Chapter Five, Remarque takes the opportunity to contemplate the war and its effects on his generation. His treatment suggests that for every terrible event there is an opposite opportunity: The comradeship that reveals the humanity of these desperate men contrasts with the terrible inhumanity all around them.

Theme

Paul counts up the men in his class that enlisted together. Of the twenty, one is insane, seven are dead, and four are wounded. Before the war, these boys sat near him in class and learned about cohesion and mathematics, subjects that do not help them now to survive. As Paul says, "We remember mighty little of all that rubbish. Anyway, it has never been the slightest use to us." This leads him to consider what will happen after the conflict ends. He tells his friends:

> . . . when I hear the word "peace-time," it goes to my head: and if it really came, I think I would do some unimaginable thing—something, you know, that it's worth having lain here in the muck for. But I can't even imagine anything. . . ."

He adds, to himself, "All at once everything seems to me confused and hopeless." And Albert replies, "The war has ruined us for everything."

Character Insight

With this hollow feeling, Remarque contrasts the comradeship of Kat and Paul. That evening in their shed, away from the deafening bombs and shrapnel and the grisly war deaths, they share a quiet moment of feasting and fellowship. Paul muses that they sit "opposite one another . . . two soldiers in shabby coats," and cook a goose in the darkness of the night. "We don't talk much, but I believe we have a more complete communion with one another than even lovers have."

Glossary

bobby [Informal] a British policeman.

court-martialled convicted by a court-marial, a trial by armed-forces personnel of a person accused of breaking military law.

"William Tell" a dramatic historical poem written by Johann Schiller in 1804, which emphasizes the themes of freedom and patriotism. In Swiss legend, William Tell was a hero in the fight for independence from Austria, forced, on pain of death, to shoot an apple off his son's head with bow and arrow.

Poetic League of Göttingen a spontaneous Göttingen University league of appreciators of romantic poetry organized in 1771, similar to the "Dead Poet's Society." By 1775, the students eventually drifted apart after many of them graduated.

Charles the Bald Charles I A.D. 823–877; king of France (843–877) and, as Charles II, Holy Roman Emperor (875–877).

the battle of Zama a reference to the Battle of Zama of 202 B.C.; in which Scipio (237?–183? B.C.), a Roman general, defeated Hannibal (247–183? B.C.), a Cathaginian general who occupied what is now Tunisia, ending the 2d Punic War.

Lycurgus real or legendary Spartan lawgiver of about the 9th century B.C.

pince-nez eyeglasses without temples, kept in place by a spring gripping the bridge of the nose.

possy a location, or position.

hop it [Brit. slang] move along quickly.

C.B. confinement to barracks.

skat a card game for three people, played with thirty-two cards.

Chapter Six

Summary

Rumors return the men's attention to a possible offensive. As they pass the shelled remains of a school, they see a hundred sweet-smelling pine coffins stacked against it, preparations for their own casualties. Nightly, the British strengthen both troops and munitions—ominous reminders that the war shows no signs of ending. Paul grows morose and superstitious about his fate after narrowly escaping death in either of two foxholes while passing from one to the other. German artillery is so worn that shells fall on German troops. Fat rodents, which the men call "corpse-rats," gnaw the men's bread. Detering makes a game of outwitting the creatures.

The law of averages seems to work against the men's chances of survival. Dispersal of Edamer cheese and rum suggests that hard times lie ahead. From nights of persistent shelling, green recruits vomit from fear, endangering the others with the spread of panic. Although no attack begins, the men grow numb from the continual din of barrage.

Paul's trench is almost obliterated by exploding shells, which also hinder the cook from transporting rations from the rear. Two parties attempt to locate food, then return empty-handed. Exhausted by the lengthy bombardment, lack of sleep, and inadequate food, the men battle insurgent rats, which scream in terror. One soldier, overcome by claustrophobia, loses control and is forcefully subdued. His reason destroyed by falling shells, he rams his head against a wall.

On the third day, heavy gunfire projects beyond Paul's dugout as the French launch an attack. The trenches, blown apart, attest to the fierceness of the fight. Like robots, the men fall back to more stable positions, surprising the Allies with fierce resistance, then plunge ahead in renewed effort. Paul sees glimpses of carnage as he rushes to capture enemy positions. He and the others, after an hour's rest, consume French rations of canned corned beef, bread, and cognac.

At nightfall, Paul clutches a dew-sprinkled gun and walks sentry duty in a cathedral courtyard under cover of mist. After the day's battle, he has difficulty recovering his composure. He allows his mind and emotions to focus on the poplar avenue, which evokes nostalgic memories of home, of innocent play: "We loved them dearly [the trees], and the image of those days still makes my heart pause in its beating." Overcome with melancholy, he longs to immerse himself in the serenity of nature, but concludes, "[W]e fear and love without hope."

As the war drags on, Paul loses his sense of time. He and the others attempt to retrieve the wounded, one of whom pleads for rescue but lies hidden from the search party. The offer of a reward for finding him fails. In searching, Albert is slightly wounded. The dying man calls faintly for a woman named Elise, then lapses into weeping. Against a backdrop of fleecy clouds, fresh winds, and blue skies, the dead putrefy, sickening the survivors with a sweetish smell.

The next day, Paul tries to comprehend why Haie joins souvenir hunters in collecting parachute silk and copper bands. The carefree larks and butterflies seem out of place in this No Man's Land. Although the cannons have stopped shelling them, spotter planes strafe them with gunfire. Eleven men die hideously. Lacking transport to proper burial sites, Paul and the others heap the dead three layers deep in shell holes.

Inexperienced recruits fail as reinforcements and die because they have no survival skills. Himmelstoss, panicked by the reality of frontline duty, nurses a slight wound until Paul forces him out of the dugout with insults and a rap on the head. At a lieutenant's order, Himmelstoss joins the others. Paul becomes disoriented. In his words, "[W]e run, we throw, we shoot, we kill, we lie about, we are feeble and spent. . . ." Paul and the other experienced infantrymen teach recruits how to use their ears to determine which projectiles are incoming and where they will land. Haie, severely wounded in the back, drags himself along, acknowledging to Paul that death is near. As autumn arrives, the line maintains its hold on the trenches, but roll call reveals that only thirty-two out of a hundred and fifty men of Second Company survive.

Commentary

Literary
Device

Chapter Six, one of the most brutal, graphic episodes, tests the men's mettle as they battle for a few yards of turf while living in vermin-ridden dugouts surrounded by hissing, gaseous cadavers. Despite Paul's friend's black humor about the coffins, the soldiers despair as Germany fails to overcome Allied forces. Paul, weighed down by combat, mentions the poplar trees, a strangely graceful, nonthreatening antithesis to the worn-out guns, which are so inaccurate that they endanger German troops. The repugnant motif of rat-hunting replicates the human image of men living in foxholes and scrabbling for food. The ignoble death of rats trapped in the gleam of a flashlight calls to mind the airman who is trapped by searchlights and gunned down. Just as Darwin's theory of survival of the fittest predicts, the rats that survive are the most aggressive—bloodthirsty enough to devour a couple of cats and a dog.

Seemingly, even warfare has no limits, as demonstrated by the savage Allied response to saw-edged bayonets, with which they mutilate German soldiers, strangling them with sawdust. The men, disenchanted with dependence on bayonets, rely on multipurpose spades, which can cleave "as far down as the chest." The detached tone of Paul's recitation of how to assault an aggressor evidences his immersion in self-preservation at any cost. Only twenty years old, he is already a grim mercenary capable of killing all adversaries, even if his "own father came over with them."

Character Insight

The counterpoint of Paul's stint of guard duty heightens the sense of loss as he tries to summon former feelings of love, innocence, and optimism, but cannot fully override the distant sound of artillery fire that triggers his siege mentality. His wistful, elegiac mood persists, forcing him to accept the fact that his generation is burned out, indifferent, emotionally stifled. He recognizes that he can go on existing, but that he will never feel fully alive again. Regretting the loss of his former self, he concludes, "I believe we are lost."

Literary Device

Paul's inability to warm his hands parallels the deaths of his comrades and foreshadows his own coming death. He decries the pitiless landscape, so pockmarked by craters that it resembles the moon, a cold heavenly body. Unable to solace his flagging spirits, he looks forward to a mug of barley soup, but the meal fails to brighten his mood. Even with blue skies and gentle breezes overhead, the earthly scene of rotting, bloated corpses sickens the men, who are incapable of interring so many dead comrades. Against this hellish backdrop flutter larks and two yellow and red butterflies, symbols of fragile beauty, which settle on the "teeth of a skull." Likewise Paul and his comrades, at one time innocent denizens of nature, perch on the rim of death, because they have no other place to rest.

Ironically, Paul, himself childlike under the tutelage of Kat, loses patience with ignorant recruits, whose presence indicates that German draft boards lack adult males to restock the fighting force. When recruits endanger themselves, Paul, playing the role of disapproving father, wants to spank them and "lead them away from here where they have no business to be." Poisonous gas leaves them hemorrhaging from ravaged lungs, and they soon die. Haie's injury, which bares a quivering lung, denies Paul the opportunity to bandage and rescue his friend. Haie, familiar with the odds against remaining alive, accepts his fate.

Glossary

Aunt Sally   name of a figure of a woman's head at which balls are thrown, as in a sideshow; a person or idea seen or set up as an easy target for criticism.

pocket-torch   [British] a flashlight.

Somme   a river in northern France, which flows past Amiens, where both sides battled in 1916 and then again in 1918. The first battle, costing a million lives, was a Pyrrhic victory, with so much loss to combatants that neither could claim advantage.

listening post   an advanced, concealed position near the enemy's lines, for detecting the enemy's movements by listening.

flame-thrower   a weapon for shooting a stream of flaming gasoline, oil, napalm, etc.

calibre   the size of a bullet or shell as measured by its diameter.

parapet   a wall or bank used to screen troops from frontal enemy fire.

shell-shock   a psychological condition characterized by anxiety, irritability, depression, etc., often occurring after prolonged combat in warfare.

storm-troops   the first wave of the infantry assault.

Stations of the Cross   a series of fourteen crosses, as along the walls of a church, typically placed above representations of the stages of Jesus' final sufferings and of his death and burial, visited in succession as a devotional exercise. The foreboding image connects Paul's wartime sufferings with Christ's final days.

waggle-top   a mortar shell that wobbles like a Roman candle as it spins to earth.

Chapter Seven

Summary

At the field depot, Second Company takes a brief, well deserved rest. They are reorganizing, in need of more than a hundred reinforcements. Himmelstoss is friendly and, because he brought Westhus back after he was wounded, Paul is kinder to him. Himmelstoss also took over the cooking from Ginger, so he brings Paul and his friends food. At rest and full of food, Paul cannot think of the front line. Instead, he recounts who is dead and wounded and tries to use humor to keep his thoughts straight. Kropp and Paul find a theatre poster from a long-since-abandoned theatre. The girls in the poster remind them of the life they had forgotten, and they look at themselves and see the many layers of civilization that are gone. Paul and the others decide to visit the delousing station.

Billeted near a canal, Paul and his friends swim naked and flirt in makeshift, broken French with three French girls. After the soldiers promise food, the girls boldly gesture toward their house and walk on. Later that night, undeterred by lack of official leave and bolstered by rum, punch, and tall tales, the men plunge into the canal, holding cigarettes in their boots as they swim on their backs to the opposite side. The girls welcome their late-night visitors, chatter in French, and share the food. Paul, disdainful of military brothels, clings to a small brunette, his mind filled with passion for the dream girl he saw on the poster. In her arms, he tries to forget the death and the terror of war.

Following their amorous episode, Paul is issued a seventeen-day pass, to be followed by training on the moors, totaling a full six weeks away from battle. Kat encourages him to try to get a job at the training camp; talking with Kat, Paul wonders whether he will ever see these comrades again. He buys his pals a round of drinks at the canteen, bids goodbye to the brunette, and then reports to the railhead for the long trip home.

Arriving on Saturday, Paul's heart trembles at the passing scene as it becomes more familiar. He takes in the street, cyclists, a subway, the mill bridge, an old tower, shops, and bare-armed laundresses. The smells of the stream draw his thoughts to memories of playing there as a boy.

He walks to his home. Weak from the emotion he feels when he hears his sister's voice, Paul leans on his rifle and weeps, then recovers his military bearing and demands a handkerchief. He perceives the frailty of his ailing mother and sits at her bedside, glad that he feels no need to converse, and presents his gifts of bread, butter, cheese, sausage, melted fat, and rice—rations that are in short supply among civilians. Paul's fearful mother questions him about wartime conditions, concerned about what she has heard. Although Paul mentions that his family was never demonstrative, he feels there is a distance, a veil that did not exist earlier. Unable to relieve his mother's illness, Paul assuages her worries with lies. Later, in the kitchen, Paul's sister informs him that his mother has suffered for several months with a recurrence of cancer.

On his way to the commandant's office, Paul fails to salute a major, who chastises him for his bad manners. Having endured the horrors of the front, Paul is angry that he should be scolded for his lack of protocol. He puts on civilian clothes that are too small for him since he has grown in the army; looking in a mirror he hardly recognizes himself. Although his mother welcomes his civilian clothes, his father wants him to wear his uniform, but Paul refuses. He can no longer communicate with his parents, and talking about the war simply worries him, because he does not want to put his fears into words.

Everything at home is so different from a year ago. His German master sees himself as an authority on the war and admonishes Paul for his short-term vision. Following his war experience, Paul has a difficult time seeing how the lives of these civilians can have any purpose, and he returns, dismayed, to his room at home. Looking at his books and papers, he realizes he cannot find his way back to his youth.

A sense of parting is now in the air. His mother is counting the days, and Paul realizes he must see Kemmerich's mother before he leaves for the training camp. Lying to the woman, he tells her Franz died instantly and is discomfited with her questions and her disbelief. Why does one death make so much difference when soldiers see so many? The night before Paul leaves, his mother comes into his room and they converse, but his thoughts are far different from his words. He wishes things could be the way they used to be, but he reassures her that it isn't so dangerous and tells her that she should not worry. Because his mother is very ill, Paul realizes he will probably never have the opportunity to tell her all that is in his heart. With these thoughts, he regrets coming home, because as long as he remained indifferent and hopeless he survived. Now he does not, cannot, feel that way.

Commentary

Character Insight

This chapter is a poignant, bittersweet reminder of what happened to Paul Bäumer's entire generation. The front provides a sharp contrast with the home that Paul later visits. At the front, the soldiers see basic needs as most important. As Paul says, "We will make ourselves comfortable and sleep, and eat as much as we can stuff into our bellies, and drink and smoke so that hours are not wasted. Life is short." His visit to the brunette is a reminder of the idealized dream girl on the theatre poster. Naked and in her arms, Paul feels strangely vulnerable, clinging to her like an island in a dangerous sea. After he leaves for home, he tries not to put the war front into words, because to be indifferent to it is what keeps him alive.

Literary Device

During Paul's leave, details of the beauty and familiarity of home and family touch his heart. He is so moved by the "golden-red light," the Dolbenberg Mountain, and his beloved poplar trees that he perceives the total picture and is moved by it "as though it were [his] mother." Symbolically, Paul passes over the bridge that separates home from the war. His military equipment removed, he looks up at the case that holds his butterfly collection, suggesting the separation between his youthful innocence and the hardened exterior he has acquired at the front.

Character Insight

Taking in the sights and smells of his home, Paul cries as he hears his sister's voice. The dirt and callousness of the front fall away, and he shows his compassion in lying to his mother about war conditions. Paul recognizes, with both his parents, that things are never going to be the same again. He can never describe to them what he is facing and his father, especially, is totally ignorant of the things Paul has witnessed as a young soldier. The gap between civilian and soldier is so immense that Paul says, "They have worries, aims, desires, that I cannot comprehend." He must lie to his mother and he must keep silent with his father. What a vast gulf divides them.

Back in his room he remembers the schoolboy he once was and looks up at his school-boy books. "I want that quiet rapture again. I want to feel the same powerful, nameless urge that I used to feel when I turned to my books." Wishing he could return to the "lost eagerness of [his] youth," he turns away, realizing that he cannot find his way back.

The chapter's most poignant scene is between Paul and his mother. Sensing that he will never see her again, Paul tries to soothe her fears and put on a stolid countenance. All the while he is thinking:

> Ah! Mother, Mother! How can it be that I must part from you? Who else is there that has any claim on me but you? Here I sit and there you are lying; we have so much to say, and we shall never say it.

With these words Remarque brings home the total sense of alienation Paul and his friends feel from home, family, clothing, books, trees, houses, bridges, and warmth. This generation is one that has lost its childhood, its dreams, its faith in a meaningful world, and its concern for the individual. As Paul heads back to the training camp, he realizes he no longer fits anywhere.

Glossary

canteen   a place outside a military camp where refreshments and entertainment are provided for members of the armed forces.

hoarding   [British] a billboard.

white-horses   whitecaps.

bon ami   [French] a good friend.

Un moment   [French] one moment.

La guerre—grand malheur—pauvres garçons   [French] The war—great unhappiness—poor boys.

Dolbenberg   a mountain outside Paul's hometown.

confectioner's   the store of a confectioner, a person whose work or business is making or selling confections or candy.

chemist   [British] a pharmacist.

whortleberries   blue or blackish edible berries with a powdery bloom.

dripping   the fat and juices that drip from roasting meat.

Herr   [German] Mr.; Sir.; a German title of respect.

Between Langemark and Bixschoote towns north and northwest of Ypres in northwest Belgium, one of the most war-ravaged communities of World War I.

beer garden an establishment that serves beer, often at an outdoor patio.

skittle-alley a narrow expanse of lawn where players roll a wooden ball at a tight arrangement of ninepins.

Froggies [Slang] the French; term of contempt or derision.

what we ought to annex that is, lands that Germany felt it had a right to claim.

johnnies [British] any men or boys.

Iron Cross a prestigious German military decoration.

Flanders region in northwest Europe, on the North Sea, including a part of northwest France and the provinces of East Flanders and West Flanders in Belgium.

one mark twenty pfennig the mark and the pfennig are monetary units of Germany.

territorial a volunteer home guard.

schnapps any strong alcoholic liquor.

pill-box a low, enclosed gun emplacement of concrete and steel.

pothooks S-shaped hooks for hanging pots or kettles over a fire.

bread fatigue kitchen duty.

C.O. commanding officer.

Chapter Eight

Summary

At the camp on the moors near the Soldiers' Home, Paul spends a month in retraining. Drill in the autumn air allows him time to enjoy juniper and birch trees and the fine sand underfoot. The joy of the outdoors plus card games and joking with other soldiers helps separate Paul from his thoughts of the inevitable return to the front. The Russian prisoner of war camp which abuts the training camp, forces him to look at a different kind of war victim, who must scavenge trash barrels for potato peelings and meager dregs, and suffer the bloody discharge of dysentery. The apathetic inmates, who look more like "meek, scolded, St. Bernard dogs" than adversaries, inspire his empathy. In exchange for bread, they trade their boots and crude carvings. Peasants tantalize the hungry prisoners by devouring bread and slices of sausage in front of the silent men.

On the last Sunday of his leave, Paul's father and sister visit him at the Soldiers' Home and they stroll the moors together. The hours are a torture to Paul because they have no subject to discuss but his mother's illness. She is now in a charity ward awaiting an operation. Paul's father is working overtime to try to pay the bills, but he is obviously worried. Paul goes with them to the train and they give him potato-cakes and jam his mother made. He considers giving the food to the Russian prisoners but remembers his mother stood painfully over a stove to cook them; feeling a little less guilty, he shares only two.

Commentary

Away from the front, Paul is able once more to appreciate nature. He basks in its beauty and tranquility and continues his steadfast denial of his own humanity. To think about that would mean death when he returns to the front. He muses on the nature of war and enemies. He reflects on the Russian prisoners: "A word of command has made these silent figures our enemies; a word of command might transform them into our friends." War here seems futile and absurd. Why does it happen? Paul begins to think the unthinkable: "I am frightened: I dare think this way no more. This way lies the abyss." To be humane is not healthy, and thoughts about fear and death will lead him to lose his nerve. There is not place for humane thoughts now.

Literary Device

The potato cakes symbolize the love of Paul's mother, who concerns herself with his deprivations. His decision to save them and share them at the front shows his appreciation for her sacrifice. In the next chapter, both the thoughts about war and the description of a mother's love are repeated and enlarged.

Glossary

Soldiers' Home   a recreation center, similar to the American U.S.O.

Chapter Nine

Summary

On his way back to Second Company, Paul goes by rail and on foot in search of its new location. He hears that his company is being sent to places "wherever it is hottest." While this is not "cheerful" news, he searches for his friends and finds he must wait two days for the company to arrive. When his friends return they appear "grey, dirty, soured, and gloomy." Paul, holding back his emotions, shares the best cakes and jam with comrades and keeps the moldy ones for himself. He hears talk of assignment to the Russian front. Clothed temporarily in new tunics, for eight days the men drill in preparation for inspection by the Kaiser. When their leader appears, Paul is disappointed that he looks like an ordinary man. After the Kaiser distributes Iron Crosses, the group talks about war and why it happens. Remarque once again shows the plight of the little man caught up in forces over which he has no control. The inspection finished, the uniforms are returned because the show is over and it is now time to get back to work.

Returning to battle, Paul, by now desensitized to macabre scenes, marches past parts of bodies hanging in trees, blown out of their uniforms by the impact of trench mortars, the blood still fresh. Paul volunteers to go out on a night patrol with his friends to check the strength of the enemy. Because he has been away from the front, this is his first retesting of his battle courage. Something falls near Paul and he panics. Telling himself that he is panicking because he is new again at the front, Paul sees and hears a hundred sounds and images in his mind: his mother's voice, Russians, wire fences, dead bodies. Covered with sweat, Paul is losing his nerve, and he cannot move from his shallow hole. Paul argues with himself to go, feeling guilt and remorse. But then he hears the voices of his company and imagines one is Kat: It is alright now, and he is fine.

Cautiously Paul leaves and snakes his way forward. Now "intelligent fear" and "heightened caution" are guiding him. Momentarily confused, he does not recognize the best direction. The light of the rockets keep him paralyzed and, as he describes it, "A shell crashes. . . . bombardment. . . . Machine-guns rattle." He has made his way, despite his fear, to a large crater and lies with his legs in water up to his belly. Soon the attack will start and he will pretend to be dead. Pulling out a small dagger just in case someone ends up in the hole with him, he senses that shells of his own side fall near him, making him furious that he might be killed by friendly fire. However, Paul realizes that if his own side makes a counter raid, he will be saved. Sure enough, they seem to repulse the attack.

Just as Paul is about to leave, a body falls on him in the dark. He strikes at it madly and it convulses and collapses. Wanting to leave, Paul must wait because machine-gun fire pins him down. Light increases and he can feel the wet, sticky blood on his hands. He wipes it off with mud and figures his company has given up on finding him. Morning light breaks and the body moves, a man with a small, pointed beard. Not dead, he is staring at Paul in terror, and Paul tries to reassure him by whispering, "No, no." Paul uses a handkerchief to collect water for the man and gives him a drink. Unbuttoning the man's tunic, Paul discovers three wounds and decides, as he bandages the man, that it is only a matter of time before the man dies. If he had a revolver, he would shoot the man mercifully, but he does not, so he must listen to the man's gasps for breath for hours. Around three o'clock in the afternoon, the man breathes his last breath, and the silence is worse than the groans. This is the first time Paul has killed a man in hand-to-hand combat. All is chance in war.

In a moment of temporary insanity, Paul speaks to the corpse. He explains that the man was merely an abstraction. But now Paul realizes, "We always see it too late." He asks the man's forgiveness because he knows now that the enemy is a flesh-and-blood man like himself. Checking the man's tunic for his name and address, Paul hesitates because a name will make the man real and will stay with Paul for the rest of his life. He finds a picture of a woman and a little girl in the man's tunic. They are obviously not rich, and Paul thinks of writing to the woman or sending her money. Finally, he resolves to live for the sake of this man, Gérald Duval, printer, and he promises that if he does come out of this, he will make sure war never happens again.

Twilight comes and, along with it, a return to temporary reason. Paul is no longer thinking about the dead man. He is recognizing instead that if he tries to return to his own company, they may shoot him accidentally. By the light of a rocket, Paul sees helmets from his own company and realizes Kat and Albert are there with a stretcher, looking for him.

The next day, Paul tells Kat and Albert about the dead printer; they assure him that he could have done nothing else. Listening to his friends, Paul calms himself and tries to rationalize the whole experience. He is finally able to forgive himself and concludes pragmatically, "After all, war is war."

Commentary

Much of Chapter Nine concerns Paul's readjustment to the front and also continues to develop Remarque's philosophy on a number of issues stemming from war. The Kaiser's visit causes Paul and his friends to discuss the nature of war and those who fight it. They wonder who is right: The French fight for their homeland and the Germans fight for theirs. So who is really right in protecting their land, and who is wrong? These wars are started by rulers like the Kaiser but the little people— the shopkeepers and the farmers—are the ones who must fight the war. So who profits from this event? The rulers and the generals gain fame, and many others profit financially. But those who must do the dirty work are the little people who have wives and families at home. Finally, Albert concludes, "The best thing is not to talk about the rotten business." Later, when Paul kills the French soldier, he promises him that he will try to live so as to bring wars to an end, thus ensuring peace for the little people.

The inhumanity of war is drummed home again and again, but in this chapter Remarque uses grotesque corpses hanging in trees to remind us of the impersonal use of mortars to kill large numbers. This depiction contrasts, of course, with Paul's horror when he kills a man face to face. The soldiers walk on through the woods of death, realizing that to stop and think about the grotesque sights will possibly cause them to lose their nerve. It is better not to see the enemy as human beings. In fact, the only thoughts that can calm the nerves and help survival are the voices of Paul's comrades: "They are more to me than life, these voices, they are more than motherliness and more than fear; they are the strongest, most comforting thing there is anywhere. . . ."

The most powerful image of this chapter is the incident in the shell hole, in which Paul comes face to face with his capacity to kill. The emotional cost weighs heavily on Paul as he listens to the rasping breath of Gérard Duval, a man no more belligerent nor bloodthirsty than he. Unable to speak, Duval's letters and photos speak for him, attesting to Paul that this corpse was once a contributing member of society—a husband, father, and skilled laborer. Once again, the voices of Paul's friends cut through his guilt, but one wonders whether Paul will ever be able to forget this personal, not statistical, horror.

Glossary

flying divisions   mobile units capable of rapid deployment wherever they are needed.

Kaiser   Wilhelm, or William II (1859–1941), emperor of Germany and king of Prussia (1888–1918), whose ambitions led Germany into a fruitless and costly war.

Hindenburg   Paul von (1847–1934); German field marshal; president of the Weimar Republic (1925–1934).

tommy   [British informal] a private in the British army.

trench mortars   any of various portable mortars for shooting projectiles at a high trajectory and short range.

parachute star-shell   a parachute carrying a light to illuminate troop movements in the dark.

Valenciennes   city in northern France, near the Belgian border, which the Germans occupied during World War I.

compositor   a typesetter.

Chapter Ten

Summary

Paul's luck appears to change when he is assigned, along with seven others, to guard a deserted village and supply dump. He is pleased to join Kat, Albert, Müller, Tjaden, Detering, and the rest, but mourns that Haie is no longer alive to share their good fortune. These few weeks are the last happy moments in the novel. Billeted in a cellar, Paul and his buddies create an "idyll" by rounding up blankets, a bed, eggs, butter, vegetables, and suckling pigs. With a homemade grater, they shred potatoes, which Paul cooks into cakes. While they are preparing their feast, the chimney smoke draws heavy enemy fire. The men quickly carry their loot to the dugout and spend the afternoon eating, drinking coffee, and smoking cigars; at six thirty, they eat supper. Throughout the night, they suffer diarrhea after gorging themselves on the rich pork and must dash outside to relieve their pained intestines.

For almost three weeks, Paul's group is glad to have a soft job, so they continue to enjoy the good life—eating, drinking, and smoking cigars. Finally, they reluctantly board a transport to the front, bearing with them a four-poster bed, chairs, mattress, blue silk canopy, lace coverlets, as well as sausages, conserves, and cigarettes. They also take with them a kitten they have been feeding. As their column is sent to evacuate a village, Kropp catches a bullet a little above the knee. Paul is wounded in the leg and arm.

Fleeing over a hedge into a mucky ditch, the men—Paul in the lead—head cross-country toward a dugout where they bind their wounds and size up their chances of recovery. A field ambulance evacuates them to a dressing station, and there they are vaccinated against tetanus. Albert worries about a leg amputation and Paul fights to keep his senses and not be chloroformed as the doctor examines him. The doctor removes shrapnel and appears to enjoy Paul's discomfort; he sets Paul's leg and informs him he will be going home. Afterward, Paul bribes the sergeant-major with cigars to keep him and Albert together.

Transferred to an eight-man ward in a Catholic hospital, Paul awakens at seven o'clock the next morning to the sound of Morning Devotion. Albert shouts an order for quiet and the men hurl objects at the door so that the sisters will close the door and leave them in peace. To the hospital inspector's questioning, Josef Hamacher, who receives special privileges because of a head injury, claims to have made the ruckus. During the night, while there is only one night sister on duty, the men ring repeatedly to report that Albert's wound is hemorrhaging.

The next morning, Albert's face has yellowed from loss of blood. After Franz Wächter, the victim of a gunshot wound in the arm, is wheeled away on a gurney, Josef informs the others about the Dying Room, a separate space adjacent to the mortuary where seriously ill patients are taken to die. By afternoon, a new patient occupies Franz's bed. Little Peter, who suffers a lung injury, cries out belligerently that he will not be dumped in the Dying Room. Solemnly, Josef predicts that they will not see Peter again.

The doctors at the hospital are portrayed as cruel and indifferent to suffering. Paul is operated on because his bones are not growing together. Josef warns him that the doctors love to operate because they have so many human guinea pigs. Eventually, more men die than will fit into the Dying Room. Then, amazingly, Peter returns from the Dying Room in triumph. Paul, overcome by the suffering around him, observes, "A hospital alone shows what war is." Albert's leg has been amputated at the thigh and he spends a great deal of time depressed, not speaking, and he says he would kill himself if given a gun. Once again Paul ponders what they will do after the war, because all they have known is killing.

Paul turns his attention to Johann Lewandowski, a Polish soldier and the oldest patient, who has suffered a serious abdominal wound. Thrilled with a letter from his wife, Marja, he longs to see her and the child who was born during his two-year absence. Propped on a pillow after Marja arrives, Johann and his wife make love while the men play skat; two other men watch for intruders and Albert tends the baby. Remarque compresses much of Paul's convalescence into the closing paragraphs. Soon, Paul returns home on leave and again regrets having to leave his mother. Return to Second Company is less comforting without the presence of Albert, his best friend, who has gone to an institution that fits prosthetic limbs.

Commentary

Theme

As Paul recovers enough to walk about the hospital, he analyzes the impact of the war from another perspective. The experience of seeing so many hideous wounds, so many groaning, dying men forces him to ponder the great waste of the war, which extends throughout Germany, France, and Russia. Speaking for Remarque, he says,

> How senseless is everything that can ever be written, done, or thought, when such things are possible. It must be all lies and of no account when the culture of a thousand years could not prevent this stream of blood being poured out, these torture-chambers in their hundreds of thousands. A hospital alone shows what war is.

Paul broadens this thought out to his entire generation, no matter what country or side in the war. How will they ever go back to a civilian life they cannot comprehend? They went directly from school to killing. They do not even know what civilian life is supposed to be like as young adults. The entire chapter is filled with despair, death, and pain; the suffering of the men in the hospitals is only assuaged by the mercy of the sisters who tend them.

One aspect of the chapter is hopeful, however. When Lewandowski's wife comes to visit with their child, she brings a ray of hope to the ward and to the story. In this shadow of death and suffering, the men join together to allow the couple some privacy so they can share their love. It is one bright bit of sunshine in a shadowy valley of gloom.

Glossary

wireless-men radio operators.

"An der Weser" "On the Weser [River]."

daisy-cutters anti-personnel shells that are fired at ground level.

Saxon a member of an ancient Germanic people of northern Germany; here, a blue-eyed, blond European.

the well-known phrase from Goethe's "Götz von Berlichingen" the reference is to the phrase "lick my ass."

chloroform a toxic liquid, with a sweet taste, used as a solvent, fumigant, etc. and here as a general anesthetic.

tea-cosy   a knitted or padded cover placed over a teapot to keep the contents hot.

clink   [Informal] a jail; prison.

commissariat   food supplies.

excreta   waste matter excreted from the body, as sweat or urine.

mantilla   a woman's scarf, as of lace, worn over the hair and shoulders.

napkin   [British] a diaper.

Chapter Eleven

Summary

Back at the front in springtime, Paul perceives war as a kind of disease, "the cause of death like cancer and tuberculosis, like influenza and dysentery." His mind refuses to focus on the carnage, which leaves craters on both the physical and emotional landscape. No one remembers what existed prior to the war, and the only fleeting enjoyment is in the brotherhood of soldiers. Life is "limited to what is most necessary," such as whether to eat in case a later belly wound would be complicated by food. Paul tries to think of the positives and hang on to them "against the onslaught of nothingness."

As time goes by, the shell between sanity and insanity is broken. The German line, buffeted into shreds, disintegrates into a "bitter struggle from crater to crater." So desperate do the men become as the English surround them that they urinate into the empty case that holds water to cool the machine gun. Detering sees a cherry tree blossoming in a garden and its reminder of wife and home cause him to desert. He is later caught and court-martialed. Berger illustrates a case of front-line madness. He leaves the crater and goes out a hundred yards to help a wounded messenger dog. Shot in the pelvis, he is brought back by a stretcher bearer who gets a leg wound. Müller is also dead. He is shot at point-blank range in the stomach and lives half an hour in terrible pain. He gives Paul his pocket-book and the boots that were worn so long ago by Kemmerich. Taking the boots, Paul grimly says that, after he himself dies, they will go to Tjaden.

Against a fresh supply of American and British adversaries, the German army bleeds its life away. The Germans are running out of shells, have too few horses, and are helpless against the new and menacing machines of war—Allied tanks. Firearms are in short supply and barrels wear down, distorting the soldiers' aim. Germany is so strapped for replacement troops that the army drafts young boys, who are of little use. Military surgeons are so eager to return men to battle that they stamp men A1 without examining them. Paul despises the "fraud, injustice, and baseness" in the army and also blames the German factory owners who are getting rich while putting sawdust in the rations, which rip out the soldiers' intestines.

Lt. Bertinck, who has served as a worthy example for two years, dies while combating a flamethrower. The shot that hits his chin veers into Leer's hip and he bleeds to death. Paul bitterly recounts, "What use is it to him now that he was such a good mathematician at school."

Spring becomes the wretched summer of 1918. Cognizant of Germany's heavy losses, Paul is keenly aware of life. His descriptions of nature allude to its natural presence amid the carnage: red poppies, smooth beetles, black and mystic trees, stars, and flowing water. Rumors of peace encourage him to hang on in hopes of an armistice. By now English and American planes outnumber Germany's fleet five to one. Paul summarizes, "We are not beaten, for as soldiers we are better and more experienced; we are simply crushed and driven back by overwhelming superior forces."

Late in summer, Kat sustains a wound to the shin. Paul shoulders his buddy and hurries toward medical help, stopping occasionally to rest and reflect on their experiences. Because the two have been friends for nearly three years, Paul requests Kat's address so that they can remain in touch when they return to civilian life. Kat's condition worsens; Paul, without realizing that Kat has received a mortal wound to the skull, staggers on toward the dressing station. The orderly pronounces Kat "stone dead." Paul's mind, unable to cope with fatigue and, more importantly, the personal loss of his best friend, goes blank.

Commentary

Literary Device

The atmosphere of the final chapters grows more desperate. The German army and its soldiers, such as Kat and Paul, appear to be totally resigned to the futility of their situation. The Western Front is collapsing and many of the soldiers, represented by Detering and Berger, dissolve into madness. The past three years of their lives have been nothing but death, gas, horror, mud, rats, brutal scenes, shelling, desperation, and madness. Remarque constantly shells the reader with all of these things, as well as with the hopelessness and futility of war in general.

Character Insight

Paul alone, out of his original group of seven classmates, has survived, and now even his remaining support, Kat, is taken away from him. The only thing helping Paul survive was the brotherhood and comradeship of his friends. Now not even that is possible, and the loss of Kat is so great that Paul (or Remarque) cannot begin to describe it.

When the orderly asks Paul if they are related, he says, "No, we are not related. No, we are not related." We see the bitter irony in his reply, because much earlier Paul said of their tie, "I belong to them and they to me; we all share the same fear and the same life, we are nearer than lovers, in a simpler, a harder way. . . ."

Glossary

gendarmes   police officers in France and Belgium.

Verey light   a flare gun.

latrine poles   poles that serve as toilet seats above holes dug to contain human excrement.

A1   a person who is fit for military service. Lesser degrees of fitness rate C3 or B3, for example.

Chapter Twelve

Summary

Now it is Autumn of 1918. All talk is of peace and an armistice. Resting for fourteen days because he swallowed some gas, Paul considers the possibility that an armistice means they can go home. But what is home? He and his whole generation have no goals, no aims, no passion for life and no direction. Sadly, Paul mentions that the generation before and after his had a civilian life as young adults; his generation does not. The days and years will pass and he will be alone without fear or hope.

Then Paul must go back to the front, alone. The narrative suddenly changes to third person as if someone else is telling the story. October 1918, a month before the armistice, Paul dies at the front; he did not suffer and there was an expression of calm on his face as though he was glad the end had come.

Commentary

Theme

As the plot moves inexorably toward a conclusion, Remarque, becoming more philosophical and less objective, omits details of Paul's gas injury, two-week leave, return to the front, and fatal wound. Even the setting of the garden in which he convalesces is ambiguous. By this point, details have receded in importance. For Paul and the other veterans, bestiality and carnage have usurped three years of their lives, leaving empty, aimless men to be the future generation of Germans. A compelling cry of abandonment, Paul's final words, "I am so alone," summarize the treachery of war, an insidious malaise that obliterates all ties with life, leaving an empty, dehumanized husk, which bears no will to live. The final bitter irony is the quiet and stillness on the day of Paul's death: ". . . the army report confined itself to the single sentence: All quiet on the Western Front."

CHARACTER ANALYSES

Paul Bäumer

Too innocent and inexperienced at first to foresee the violent shift in his thinking, Paul, whose last name comes from the German word for *tree*, must learn to bend and sway with violent forces in order to remain firmly rooted in reality and to survive the inhuman buffeting that besets the German army. His thought processes are continually pulled to and fro, from the romantic notions of war he learned in school to the horrific lessons he absorbs through war's random destruction of his friends. Not capable of Müller's pragmatism, Paul nonetheless adapts to war and passes along the training he gains from Kat and from personal experience to the raw recruit who does not respond quickly enough to poisonous gas. Paul's delicacy and understanding extends to advice about tossing away underpants soiled by the young soldier during his first bombardment. The reader assumes that Paul himself has endured such unbridled terror and loss of bodily control.

Two years into the war, Paul, at age twenty, feels "cut off from activity, from striving, from progress" and acknowledges that he no longer believes in the values he once held dear. Impotent before the grinding, relentless war machine, like the rats he and the others kill, he races from cover to cover, protecting himself and avenging himself on the faceless enemy. Along the way, he is cut off from friends who are savagely destroyed. As with Haie, Paul can do little more than be there and wait for death to end the agony. He admits that he comes from an undemonstrative family of toilers, but his instinctive compassion for others often surfaces, particularly when comrades on whom he depends sustain wounds and when their deaths move him to sincere grief.

Returned home on furlough, Paul tries to reignite his enthusiasm for books; however, the effort is futile. His mind is so overcharged with front-line survivalist instincts that he is unable to reconnect with the simple idealism common to adolescence. After his harrowing experience with hand-to-hand combat and sharing a shell crater with a corpse, Paul embraces comradeship as his one salvation. Later, recovering in the Catholic hospital, he comments: "I am young, I am twenty years old; yet I know nothing of life but despair, death, fear, and fatuous superficiality cast over an abyss of sorrow." He concludes that he has prepared himself for the business of killing and wonders, "What will happen afterwards?" By Chapter Eleven, he is reduced to the bare bones of survival.

Himmelstoss

The former postman, whose name means "heaven-knocker," overexerts his authority and is reported by the son of a local magistrate. As a result, the tormentor is sent to the front to fight alongside the men he intimidated with his petty drills and sadistic punishments. Adorned with a twitching red mustache and aware that his role as drill instructor leaves him open to a vengeful shot in the back, he opens the way for insubordination by pressing veteran soldiers for meaningless parade-ground courtesies. Paul labels Himmelstoss' zealotry a "raging book of army regulations."

The comeuppance for Himmelstoss provides the novel with a rare instance of poetic justice. After a drubbing by Tjaden and his pals, Himmelstoss continues to lord his authority through complaint to the commandant. His strutting ends when he faces a bombardment that kills officer and recruit alike. To his cowering, Paul pours out abuse:

> "You lump, will you get out—you hound, you skunk, sneak out of it, would you?" His eyes become glassy, I knock his head against the wall—"You cow"—I kick him in the ribs—"You swine"—I push him toward the door and shove him out head first.

Himmelstoss, jolted from his panic by a lieutenant's orders, regains his professionalism and becomes "the smart Himmelstoss of the parade-ground," passing up the lieutenant in his zeal to make a good impression.

Remarque allows Himmelstoss a reprieve from ignominy in Chapter Seven, after he replaces Ginger the cook. Paul acknowledges that not only has the group's former nemesis carried Haie back from the front, but has begun spreading favors among the men. Treats in the canteen, sugar and butter from the kitchen, and easy jobs peeling potatoes and turnips combine with "real officers' fare," the enticement that vengeful soldiers cannot refuse.

Franz Kemmerich

Although Kemmerich appears in only two chapters of the book, his wartime experience makes the first strong impression of ill fate, suffering, and loss. As Paul and his friends visit him, they perceive the real truth about war; he lies on bed 26, incapable of sensing the amputation of his foot. During Paul's hour-long last visit to his friend,

Kemmerich, unwilling to accept false hope, frets that he will soon die. Childlike in size and teary-eyed in response to death in so makeshift a place, he expires in ragged gasps, leaving undried tears on his cheeks. For Paul and his buddies, Franz is the first face-to-face warning of hard times to come.

On furlough, Paul maintains his loyalty to Franz by facing the boy's mother. Having witnessed her humiliating display of motherly affection when Franz departed for the front, Paul knows that she will not accept her son's death with grace. To spare her further pain, he concocts a scenario in which Franz dies instantly. The lie, prophetic of Paul's death, epitomizes a dignified exit that any soldier would prefer to the ragged, agonizing demise of Haie, Tjaden, Kat, Berger, Gérard Duval, Johann Lewandowski, and other mangled sufferers.

Albert Kropp

A contemplative man, Albert, who curses Kemmerich's ill fate, turns over in his mind the significance of his experiences and concludes that wars would be fair if warmongers met in a ring and fought like toreador and bull, using only clubs as weapons. In Chapter Five, as the men contemplate a return to civilian life, he labels them useless and assumes that they will probably all die in battle. Although he lacks the fire of Tjaden, the flexibility of Kat, and the wistful longing of Detering, he possesses enough spirit to aid Paul in humiliating Himmelstoss by spilling excrement on the drill instructor's legs, thus ending the tyrannical martinet's cruel torments. A cheerful humanist at heart, Kropp joins search parties who seek out the dying. For his efforts, he has his ear lobe shot off. When Paul leaves for six weeks, Albert accompanies him to the station to bid him good luck.

After being wounded above the knee, Albert vows that he will kill himself before living life without his leg, which is amputated at thigh level. Perhaps as object lesson, a musician who shares his ward tries to stab himself in the heart with a fork, driving in the tines with blows from his shoe. Eventually, Albert, grudging and tight-lipped, comes to accept his loss and takes part in the ward's welcome of Marja Lewandowski. As an example of his physical and emotional healing, Albert has improved enough to baby-sit the Lewandowski child. Parted from Paul, Albert says little about the next phase of convalescence—learning to cope with an artificial leg.

Leer

The first of Paul's class to experience intercourse, Leer lords his insider's knowledge over the other men by recounting his conquests. The leader in flirtation with local women, he locates their house and joins the group who swim the canal. Fearless of the possibility that the women may be courted by officers, he concludes that no one can read their regimental numbers in the twilight. Endowed with a gluttonous appetite, he pantomimes eating before actively romancing the blonde Frenchwoman. After growing a beard, Leer seems twice his age. During the worst of Germany's battering, he receives a wound that tears open his hip, quickly spilling his blood. Ironically, it is the same bullet that tears through Lt. Bertink's chin. Paul watches Leer collapse like an empty tube and wonders what use his mathematical skills were to him in the end.

Kat

The master scrounger, who even secures four boxes of lobsters to share with his comrades, lightens the load of the young combatants by removing their dependence on the military and reconnecting them with the earth and the normal order of hustling for a good meal, a manly jest, and an untroubled sleep. Kat is an experienced, cool-headed warrior who once survived two days behind enemy lines in Russia before making his way back to his unit. After the bombardment of the cemetery, Kat, like a comforting father, sits near Paul and eases him from the nightmare. As they leave the wreckage left in the cemetery, Kat suggests shooting the young recruit, whose terrible wounds will surely kill him.

On the way to the aid station, Paul, who must carry Kat because he cannot locate a stretcher, ponders his love for the older man:

> Kat my friend, Kat with the drooping shoulders and
> the poor, thin moustache, Kat, whom I know as I know
> no other man, Kat with whom I have shared these years—
> it is impossible that perhaps I shall not see Kat again.

Because of his son-like devotion to Kat during their three years together, Paul writes down Kat's address and even considers shooting himself in the foot so that they may remain together at the aid station. After Kat dies from a shrapnel splinter in the head, the loss of "Militiaman Stanislaus Katczinsky" seems all the more intolerable, as though the final prop has been knocked from beneath Paul, leaving him defenseless in the face of the interminable war.

Gérard Duval

By a chance landing into the watery foxhole that Paul inhabits, Gérard Duval falls victim to Paul's small dagger. The Frenchman, with his pointed beard and gurgling, dying breath, rivets Paul's attention, pulling him on "a terrible journey of three yards, a long, a terrible journey" until Paul arrives at his side. Paul's perusal of the man at close range reaffirms earlier inferences about war: The enemy is composed of ordinary men, like the Russian prisoners of war, who hold no personal grudge against German soldiers.

Unable to cry out, Duval seems even more pitiable because of his terrified expression and his inability to speak. After his death around three o'clock in the afternoon, Paul learns more about Duval by rummaging through his wallet, locating letters and pictures of his family, and learning that he worked as a typesetter. Paul regrets the death, noting "the dead man might have had thirty more years of life if only I had impressed the way back to our trench more sharply on my memory." The crazed monologue continues, with Paul vowing to write to Duval's wife, begging forgiveness, and seeking an illogical atonement by promising to become a printer.

The confrontation with Duval creates a resolve in Paul to "fight against this, that has struck us both down; from you, taken life—and from me—? Life also." The next morning, safely returned by Kat and Albert, Paul pours out the story of Duval's death. He is reminded, "That is what you are here for."

CRITICAL ESSAYS

Major Themes

In the autumn of 1918, Paul Bäumer, a 20-year-old German soldier, contemplates his future: "Let the months and years come, they can take nothing from me, they can take nothing anymore. I am so alone and so without hope that I can confront them without fear" (Chapter Twelve). These final, melancholy thoughts occur just before his young and untimely death. In *All Quiet on the Western Front*, Erich Maria Remarque creates Paul Bäumer to represent a whole generation of men who are known to history as the "lost generation." Eight million men died in battle, twenty-one million were injured, and over six and a half million noncombatants were killed in what is called "The Great War." When the smoke cleared and the bodies were finally buried, the world asked—like Paul and his friends—why? Remarque writes his story to explain their reason for asking this question and why they felt betrayed by their teachers, families, and government. He creates a tale of inhumanity and unspeakable horror and the only redeeming themes of his book are the recurring ideas of comradeship in the face of death and nature's beauty in the face of bleak hopelessness.

The lost generation

Remarque prefaces his story with his purpose: "I will try simply to tell of a generation of men who, even though they may have escaped shells, were destroyed by the war." Throughout the story, the reader feels that this generation has come through an event that closes forever their chance to go back to the world of their childhood. As early as Chapter Two, Paul Bäumer describes the difference between his generation and that of his parents or even the older soldiers. They had a life before the war, a life where they felt comfortable and secure. But Paul's generation never had a chance at that life. He explains, "Our knowledge of life is limited to death" (Chapter Ten). Even when the story begins, all Paul has known is death, horror, fear, suffering, and hopelessness. He and his fellow classmates are only nineteen and twenty years old; even the young recruit who is mortally wounded in Chapter Four causes Kat to say, "Such a kid. . . .young innocents—." They feel nothing, believe in nothing, and see no future because of their experiences in the war.

Even if there were a future, in Chapter Five, Paul and his friends occasionally speculate on what it might hold. Paul cannot imagine anything that would have been "worth having lain here in the muck for" and sees everything as "confused and hopeless." His friend Albert, who will end up in a hospital with his leg amputated, feels that the war has ruined them for everything. Another soldier in their group, Kropp, understands that they will not be able to peel away two years of shells and bombs like an old sock When they were eighteen, they were just starting to live life as adults, but that life was cut short by the war and, as Paul says of their world, ". . . we had to shoot it to pieces. The first bomb, the first explosion, burst in our hearts." Will they live to fall in love, to marry, to have children? This is a future they cannot imagine and dare not think about.

Paul goes home on leave and regrets what it does to his heart. As he enters his childhood town, he realizes his life will never be the same. A terrible gulf exists between his present and his past and also between himself and his parents. He sees his past, in Chapter Six, as "a vast inapprehensible melancholy. . . . They [memories] are past, they belong to another world that is gone from us. . . . And even if these scenes of our youth were given back to us we would hardly know what to do. . . . I believe we are lost." At home on leave among his books and childhood papers, he realizes that he can never find his way back to that earlier Paul. Too much has happened at the front for him to believe in human beings or compassion. Even with his parents he realizes that life will never be the same. Paul knows his contemporaries share his feelings near the end of his story when he views the desperate and dying in the hospital: ". . . [a]nd all men of my age, here and over there, throughout the whole world see these things; all my generation is experiencing these things with me."

Betrayal

This lost generation felt a terrible sense of betrayal by their parents, teachers, and government. As they looked around and asked "why," they focused on what they had learned at home and in school. Paul and his friends feel a terrible sense of the absurd when they see how important protocol seems to be to the older generation. The Kaiser visits and all is polished until he leaves; then the new uniforms are given back and the rags of uniforms reappear. The patriotic myths of the older generation become apparent when Paul goes home. A sergeant-major chastises Paul for not saluting him when Paul has spent a good share of his life in the trenches killing the enemy and trying to survive. These examples of betrayal appear again and again in Remarque's novel.

Parents also carry the heavy burden of the lost generation's accusation. Paul says that German parents are always ready with the word "coward" for a young person who will not join up. He feels that parents should have been mediators and guides for Paul's friends, but they let them down. No longer can they trust their parents' generation. He speaks of the wise but poor people in relation to their parents: "The wisest were just the poor and simple people. They knew the war to be a misfortune, whereas those who were better off, and should have been able to see more clearly what the consequences would be, were beside themselves with joy." He sees this already in Chapter One and realizes that his generation is terribly alone and does not share its parent's traditional values.

Teachers are also to blame. Going home, Paul hears the head-master spew empty patriotic rhetoric and argue that he knows better than Paul what is happening in the war. Paul blames his old schoolteacher Kantorek for Joseph Behm's death, because Kantorek goaded the hapless Behm to join up. And Paul knows there are Kantoreks all over Germany lecturing their students to patriotic fervor. Even Leer, who was so good at mathematics in school, dies of a terrible wound and Paul wonders what good his school-learned mathematics will do him now. Paul's entire generation has a terrible feeling of betrayal when they consider military protocol, their parents, and their school teachers.

Old men start the war and young men die. Whether it be this war or any war since, the agony of the fighters is echoed in Paul's words in Chapter Ten, as he gazes around the hospital:

> And this is only one hospital, one single station; there are hundreds of thousands in Germany, hundreds of thousands in France, hundreds of thousands in Russia. How senseless is everything that can ever be written, or done, or thought, when such things are possible. It must be all lies and of no account when the culture of a thousand years could not prevent this stream of blood being poured out, these torture-chambers in their hundreds of thousands. A hospital alone shows what war is.

Man's inhumanity to man

Paul and his friends become so inured to death and horror all around them that the inhumanity and atrocities of war become part of everyday life. Here is where Remarque is at his greatest: in his description of the true horror and paralyzing fear at the front. He describes the atrocities, the terrible consequences of weapons of mass destruction, and how soldiers become hardened to death and its onslaught of sensory perceptions during battle.

Atrocities are simply a part of the inhumane business of war. In Chapter Six, Paul and his men come across soldiers whose noses are cut off and eyes poked out with their own saw bayonets. Their mouths and noses are stuffed with sawdust so they suffocate. This constant view of death causes the soldiers to fight back like insensible animals. They use spades to cleave faces in two and jab bayonets into the backs of any enemy who is too slow to get away. Their callousness is contrasted with the reaction of the new recruits who sob, tremble, and give in to frontline madness described over and over again in scenes of the front.

Remarque vividly recounts the horror of constant death as Paul comes upon scenes of destruction. In Chapter Six, he sees a Frenchman who dies under German fire. The man's body collapses, hands suspended, and then his body drops away with only the stumps of arms and hands hanging in the wire and the rest of his body on the ground. They later come upon a scene with dead bodies whose bellies are swollen like balloons. "They hiss, belch, and make movements. The gases in them make noises." The smell of blood and putrefaction is overwhelming and causes many of Paul's company to be nauseated and retch. The assault on the senses is overwhelming. They later pile the dead in a shell hole with "three layers so far." This horrifying picture is grimly elaborated on in Chapter Nine when they pass through a forest where there are bodies of victims of trench mortars. It is a "forest of the dead." Parts of naked bodies are hanging in trees, and Paul brutally describes pieces of arms here and half of a naked body there.

By the time Remarque reaches Chapter Eleven, he has described the soldier's life as one long, endless chain of the following:

> Shells, gas clouds, and flotillas of tanks—shattering, corroding, death. Dysentery, influenza, typhus—scalding, choking death. Trenches, hospitals, the common grave— there are no other possibilities.

Comradeship

Throughout all the horrifying pictures of death and inhumanity, Remarque does scatter a redeeming quality: comradeship. When Paul and his friends waylay Himmelstoss and beat on him, we laugh because he deserves it and they are only giving him his due. As time goes by, however, the pictures of camaraderie relieve the terrible descriptions of front line assaults and death, and they provide a bright light in a place of such terrible darkness. A young recruit becomes gun-shy in his first battle when a rocket fires and explosions begin. He creeps over to Paul and buries his head in Paul's chest and arms, and Paul kindly, gently, tells him that he will get used to it (Chapter Four).

Perhaps the two most amazing scenes of humanity and caring can be found in the story of the goose roasting and the battle where his comrades' voices cause Paul to regain his nerve. In Chapter Five, Paul and Kat have captured a goose and are roasting it late at night. Paul says, "We don't talk much, but I believe we have a more complete communion with one another than even lovers have. We are two men, two minute sparks of life; outside is the night and the circle of death." As he watches Kat roasting the goose and hears his voice, it brings Paul peace and reassurance. Over and over again, in scenes of battle and scenes of rest, we see the comradeship of this tiny group of men. Even though Paul counts their losses at various points, he always considers their close relationship and attempts to keep them together to help each other. In Chapter Nine, when Paul is alone in the trench, he loses his nerve and his direction and is afraid he will die. Instead, he hears the voices of his friends: "I belong to them and they to me; we all share the same fear and the same life; we are nearer than lovers, in a simpler, a harder way; I could bury my face in them in these voices, these words that have saved me and will stand by me." There is a grace here, in the face of all sorrow and hopelessness, a grace that occurs when men realize their humanity and their reliance on others.

Through thick and thin, battle and rest, horror and hopelessness, these men hold each other up. Finally, Paul has only Kat and he loses even this friend and father-figure in Chapter Eleven. Kat's death is so overwhelming and so final that we do not hear Paul's reaction; we only see him break down in the face of it. There is such final irony in the medic's question about whether they are related. This man, this hero, this father, this life—has been closer to Paul than his own blood relatives and yet Paul must say, "No, we are not related." It is the final stunning blow before Paul must go on alone.

Nature

Throughout his novel, Remarque uses nature in several ways. It revitalizes the soldiers after terrible hardships, reflects their sadness, and provides a contrast to the unnatural world of war. When Kemmerich, the first of Paul's classmates dies, Paul takes his identification tags and walks outside. "I breathe as deep as I can, and feel the breeze in my face, warm and soft as never before." Many times throughout the novel Remarque uses nature in this way to restore men and help them go on.

Nature also reflects the terrible sadness of the lost generation. In Chapter Four, Paul's company sustains heavy losses and a recruit is wounded so badly Paul and Kat consider killing him to end his suffering. The lorries and medics arrive too quickly, and they are forced to rethink their decision. Paul watches the rain fall and says: "It falls on our heads and on the heads of the dead, up in the line, on the body of the little recruit with the wound that is so much too big for his hip; it falls on Kemmerich's grave; it falls in our hearts." The cleansing rain falls upon the hopelessness of Paul's life and the lives of those around him. Throughout Remarque's book, we also see a strong affinity between nature and lost dreams and memories. When Paul is on sentry duty in Chapter Six, he remembers his childhood and thinks about the poplar avenue where such a long time ago they sat beneath the trees and put their feet in the stream. Back then the water was fragrant, the wind melodious; these memories of nature cause a powerful calmness and awaken a remembrance of what was—but sadly, will never be again.

Finally, butterflies play gracefully and settle on the teeth of a skull; birds fly through the air in a carefree pattern. This is nature in the midst of death and destruction. While men kill each other and wonder why, the butterflies, birds, and breeze flutter though the killing fields and carry on as if mankind were quite insignificant. Even at the end when Paul knows there is so little time until the armistice, he reflects on the beauty of life and hopes that he can stay alive until the laws of nature once again prevail and the actions of men bring peace. He describes the red poppies, meadows, beetles, grass, trees at twilight, and the stars. How can such beauty go on in the midst of such heartache?

Remarque says that this novel "will try simply to tell of a generation of men who, even though they may have escaped shells, were destroyed by the war." If words can touch what men hold to be dear in their hearts and so cause them to change the world, this book with its words of a lost generation, lost values, and lost humanity is surely one that should be required reading for all generations.

Style

Remarque, telling his story for the most part in first-person until he briefly adopts third-person following Paul's death, enables the reader to identify with a single eyewitness account, which evolves from his own experiences on the western front. Immature and at times bewildered, Paul, still in his teens, enters the war with enthusiasm, unprepared for the total obliteration of his comrades, his country's militaristic aims, his ideals, and his own fragile hold on life. As did the painters of the late nineteenth century, Remarque uses fragmented, dramatic moments in Paul's enlightenment and molds them into a stark, impressionistic whole. The most theatrical of these moments are:

- Kemmerich's dying words

- the bombardment of the cemetery

- Paul's first furlough

- the pathos of hungry prisoners

- Gérard Duval's death

- Paul's attempt to save Kat

These scenes give readers a sense of immediacy, as though they too honed bayonets, huddled in trenches, ducked waggle-tops and daisy-cutters, and grasped at life amid chaos. Taken as a unit, or what psychologists call a *gestalt*, the novel converges into a bleak pattern delineating the loss of personhood under the continual pounding of artillery, planes, and Allied assault.

Like Homer, Virgil, and the epic writers who produced the *Chanson de Roland, Mahabharata, Beowulf, Kalevala, El Cid,* and the *Nibelungenlied*, Remarque emulates the conventions of war literature, particularly the Greek epic.

He centers on the battlefield, beginning in medias res, or in the middle of things, moving back to the classroom and forward to the bitter end of Paul and his friends.

He emphasizes the Homeric, or epic simile, comparing events of war with scenes from nature, as with Paul's absorption in the coming of autumn, the rustling of poplar leaves, and "the canteens [which] hum like beehives with rumours of peace."

He catalogs his warriors, introducing Paul's classmates one by one, delineating their personality traits and idiosyncrasies, such as Detering's interest in farming, Haie's ham-sized hands, and Albert's desire to reason through the illogic of war.

He stresses hubris, the Greek concept of excessive pride, as seen in Himmelstoss' enjoyment of his power over young recruits and Kantorek's strutting chauvinism.

He depicts Paul as the vulnerable infantryman, whose importance to the world cataclysm lifts him to the level of an everyman.

He extends his canvas over a vast setting—the Western Front, which is described as a five-hundred-mile human wall pitted against the Allied assault.

He celebrates male bonding, just as the *Iliad* emphasizes Achilles' love for Patroclus, whose death overpowers his control of emotions.

He focuses on blind chance, over which humans have no power.

He maintains an objectivity toward the slaughter of a war, the proportions of which involve a long list of nations that mirror the suffering experienced by all soldiers—German or otherwise, even enemies.

In terms of the central intelligence, the novel veers sharply away from epic tradition of the noble warrior; instead, it depicts the decimation of the ordinary foot soldier. Remarque's uncanny grasp of mental breakdown suggests a personal involvement with the character—an identification stemming from his own need to exorcise the terrors of war, which, ten years after his military service, continued to plague him. In telling the story of Paul Bäumer, a German soldier, Remarque creates a universal portrayal of warfare in all its grimness and hypocrisy, despair and waste. As Paul explains his role in the Great War:

> We loved our country as much as they; we went courageously into every action; but also we distinguished the false from true, we had suddenly learned to see. And we saw that there was nothing of their world left. We were all at once terribly alone; and alone we must see it through.

Dramatizing only one enemy soldier by name and personality, Remarque concentrates on enemy fire as though it were a faceless, demonic machine, churning relentlessly through lines of men, flattening them in foxholes, skewering them with lethal projectiles from machine guns, rifles, grenades, and flamethrowers, and anonymously searing their lungs with gas. A far cry from the romanticized chivalric hero of Arthurian legends, the inexperienced young soldier, lacking epic stature, epitomizes a humanity that demands an end to international conflict acted out with heinous killing machines.

As Paul concludes, the level to which he and his comrades are reduced reminds him of Bushmen, the primitive forebears of the human race who should long before have educated future generations on the futility of war.

In Paul's only face-to-face confrontation with the enemy, he rises above savagery through first-hand experience and compassion. He speaks the apology of humankind—words that beg pardon for citizenship in nations that choose to annihilate each other rather than to negotiate peacefully their differences. Tragically, men like the Russian prisoners, Paul, Tjaden, Kat, Lewandowski, and Gérard Duval come from ordinary working class families, not the privileged, noble houses of the Kaiser or Hindenburg, whom Paul and Albert blame for fostering such wasteful destruction, such blatant disregard for nature.

Sacrifice, exemplified by the jar of jam and potato-cakes from home, falls heavily on noncombatants like Paul's mother and sister, who suffer rationing, but willingly pay the price if their self-denial means that Paul will know some bit of comfort in his mud-floored trench. Likewise, Marja abdicates the dignity of sexual relations exchanged in the privacy of her marital bed in order to snatch a few moments of intimacy with her husband, Johann, in a hospital ward. The nurse on the train, speaking for other noncombatants willing to share the privations of war, urges Paul to rest while he can and disregard the soiling of sheets, which she will gladly wash and iron in exchange for his brief enjoyment of a real bed.

Symbolism

All Quiet demonstrates a controlled use of symbols, which guide the reader's thinking toward significant themes of loss and longing.

Most prominent are the soft airman's boots, which pass from man to man after each wearer succumbs to a violent death. Worn by Kemmerich before his injury, they were undoubtedly stripped from a downed British airman before changing hands, which they do twice more as successive owners die. In all, four men possess the boots; none survives the war. In graphic scenes, Russian prisoners exchange their boots for crusts of bread; dismembered bodies lose not only boots, but the feet and legs they cover. Others, like Albert, have their limbs surgically removed, then fitted with artificial limbs, which mock the propriety of a whole body, undefiled by war.

A second symbol, butterflies, derives in part from Remarque's childhood hobby of collecting insects and mounting them in a case. For Paul, the butterflies, mocked by the ominous observation balloons that hover overhead, exemplify the innocence and joy of nature. Even when the graceful creatures alight on a skull, their presence reminds the men and the reader that the land on which battles are fought still contains a semblance of natural order. A second purpose of butterflies is a tangible representation of fragility and vulnerability. Like the frail-winged insect, Paul's life, and the lives of countless other young men, hovers on earth for a short while and ends all too soon.

The horses of Chapter Four emphasize the change of warfare from earlier dependence on beasts of burden to mechanical devices, such as grenades, cannons, flamethrowers, machine guns, balloons, and aerial shells. The noble animals, which bear a column of men to the front, remind Paul of the steeds ridden by knights of old. The terrible cries of these wounded beasts are like the "mourning of the world martyred creation, wild with anguish, filled with terror and groaning." Emblematic of the violence human warriors do to nature, the horses' terrified cries perturb Detering, the farmer who values the animals far too much to jeopardize their lives in battle. In similar fashion, the messenger dog, also victimized and left to howl its pain, draws Berger into harm's way, where he too dies in No Man's Land.

Women in the novel represent peace, gentleness, and nurturing, as well as sexual release. The girl in the poster inspires a nostalgic urge for peacetime in Paul and, for two of his comrades, she rouses them to masturbation. At the same time, the vision of her fresh good looks emphasizes Paul's scruffy clothes and infestation with lice. The brunette, who pragmatically exchanges sex for food and cigarettes, holds him close, allowing intimacy as a means of staying alive. His hometown looks so inviting that he compares it to a mother. Before reaching his front door, he rejects the offer of coffee from a smiling Red Cross sister, then gratefully accepts potato-cakes and whortleberry jam from his mother and sister, who have sacrificed to provide his favorite foods. Even at the beer garden, the spire of St. Margaret's Church seems to raise a blessing over his furlough and assure his safety for the duration of his leave. On his way out of his mother's room, Paul trips over his pack, a significant fall, which jerks his awareness back to the war, which stands in the way of his home duties, which urge him to comfort his mother as she battles cancer.

On the train to Cologne, Paul receives the kindness of a nurse who ennobles his sacrifices for his country with clean sheets and personal care. At the Catholic hospital, the nuns pray during Morning Devotion, despite the men's wish for an extended sleep. A night nurse, rousted by insistent wardmates, scurries to the aid of Albert, whose wound has broken open and begun to bleed. Another nun, Sister Libertine, spreads cheer among the men, who repay her goodness with deep gratitude, especially after she returns Little Peter from almost certain death in the room beside the morgue. Marja Lewandowski, who brings along her child, shares pieces of sausage, and plumps up wilted pillows, represents motherhood and wifely regard for her husband, who craves intercourse with her after ten months in the hospital.

Paul's fondness for potato-cakes, a direct offshoot of his attitude toward his mother, symbolizes home and sacrifice. Like the men who dig into the earth with shovels and sometimes teeth and fingernails to survive bombardment, the potato is a grubby, humble outgrowth of the same soil, as well as a welcome treat when grated and cooked in patties. During the severe rationing at home, Paul's sister must stand in line for food, his father works late to support his household, and Paul's mother, saintly and unselfish, cooks the cakes and puts up whortleberry jam because they are his favorite foods. The gifts are so precious to Paul that he feels compelled to share them with the starving prisoners of war and with his buddies.

Rhetorical Devices

Remarque demonstrates a mastery of language, which he manipulates to suit rapid shifts of tone, characterization, and theme, depending on his varying needs for graphic, blunt description, lyricism, dialogue, or lament. Passages illustrating these rhetorical devices are listed in the following sections.

Humor

- "Then [the sergeant major] steams off with Himmelstoss in his wake."

- "My arms have grown wings and I'm almost afraid of going up into the sky, as though I held a couple of captive balloons in my fists."

Personification

- "The wind plays with our hair; it plays with our words and thoughts."

- "Darknesses blacker than the night rush on us with giant strides, over us and away."

- "Over us Chance hovers."

Euphemism

- "At the same time he ventilates his backside."

- "All at once he remembers his school days and finishes hastily: 'He wants to leave the room, sister.'"

Imagery

- "To no man does the earth mean so much as to the soldier. When he presses himself down upon her long and powerfully, when he buries his face and his limbs deep in her from the fear of death by shell-fire, then she is his only friend, his brother, his mother; he stifles his terror and his cries in her silence and her security; she shelters him and releases him for ten seconds to live, to run, ten seconds of life; receives him again and often forever."

- "The front is a cage in which we must await fearfully whatever may happen."

- "I recognize the characteristic outline of the Dolbenberg, a jagged comb, springing up precipitously from the limits of the forests."

Repetition

- "Earth!—Earth!—Earth!"

- "Dawn approaches without anything happening—only the ever-lasting, nerve-wracking roll behind the enemy lines, trains, trains, lorries, lorries; but what are they concentrating?"

Antithesis

- "A man dreams of a miracle and wakes up to loaves of bread."

- "It is as though formerly we were coins of different provinces; and now we are melted down, and all bear the same stamp."

Parallel construction

- "My feet begin to move forward in my boots, I go quicker, I run."

- "The wood vanishes, it is pounded, crushed, torn to pieces."

- "No longer do we lie helpless, waiting on the scaffold, we can destroy and kill, to save ourselves, to save ourselves and to be revenged."

Simile

- "Like a big, soft jelly-fish, [gas] floats into our shell-hole and lolls there obscenely."

- "He had collapsed like a rotten tree."

Metaphor

- "When Kat stands in front of the hut and says: 'There'll be a bombardment,' that is merely his own opinion; but if he says it here, then the sentence has the sharpness of a bayonet in the moonlight, it cuts clean through the thought, it thrusts nearer and speaks to this unknown thing that is awakened in us, a dark meaning—'There'll be a bombardment.'"

■ "Immediately a second [searchlight] is beside him, a black insect is caught between them and tries to escape—the airman."

■ "I don't know whether it is morning or evening, I lie in the pale cradle of the twilight, and listen for soft words which will come, soft and near—am I crying?"

Liturgical prose

■ "Our being, almost utterly carried away by the fury of the storm, streams back through our hands from thee, and we, thy redeemed ones, bury ourselves in thee, and through the long minutes in a mute agony of hope bite into thee with our lips!"

■ "The evening benediction begins."

Apostrophe

■ ". . . dark, musty platoon huts, with the iron bedsteads, the chequered bedding, the lockers and the stools! Even you can become the object of desire."

■ "Ah! Mother, Mother! You still think I am a child—why can I not put my head in your lap and weep?"

Allusion

■ "The gun emplacements are camouflaged with bushes against aerial observation, and look like a kind of military Feast of the Tabernacles."

■ "The guns and the wagons float past the dim background of the moonlit landscape, the riders in their steel helmets resemble knights of a forgotten time; it is strangely beautiful and arresting."

Hyperbole

■ "They are more to me than life, these voices, they are more than motherliness and more than fear; they are the strongest, most comforting things there is anywhere: they are the voices of my comrades."

■ "In the evening we are hauled on to the chopping-block."

Rhetorical question

■ "Why have I always to be strong and self-controlled?"

■ "If one wants to appraise it, it is at once heroic and banal—but who wants to do that?"

Aphorism

■ "No soldier outlives a thousand chances."

■ ". . . terror can be endured so long as a man simply ducks—but it kills, if a man thinks about it."

Symbolism

■ "The national feeling of the tommy resolves itself into this—here he is."

■ "I pass over the bridge, I look right and left; the water is as full of weeds as ever."

Foreshadowing

■ "'I can sleep enough later,' she says. . . . Her face is a white gleam in the darkness."

■ "On the landing I stumble over my pack, which lies there already made up because I have to leave early in the morning."

Doggerel

- "Give 'em all the same grub and all the same pay."

- "And the war would be over and done in a day."

Short utterances

- "It is not fear."

- "Thirty-two men."

- "Life is short."

Cause and effect

- "Our faces are neither paler nor more flushed than usual; they are not more tense nor more flabby—and yet they are changed."

- "They have taken us farther back than usual to a field depot so that we can be re-organized."

Irony

- "The shells begin to hiss like safety-valves—heavy fire—. . . ."

- ". . . a high double wall of yellow, unpolished, brand-new coffins. They still smell of resin, and pine, and the forest."

Appositive

- "Thus momentarily we have the two things a soldier needs for contentment: good food and rest."

- "I have killed the printer, Gérard Duval."

Caesura

■ "It is all a matter of habit—even the front-line."

■ "The days, the weeks, the years out here shall come back again, and our dead comrades shall then stand up again and march with us, our heads shall be clear, we shall have a purpose, and so we shall march, our dead comrades beside us, the year at the Front behind us—against whom, against whom?"

■ "Pen-holders, a shell as a paper-weight, the ink-well—here nothing is changed."

Onomatopoeia

■ "The man gurgles."

■ ". . . smash through the johnnies and then there will be peace."

■ "'Heathen,' she chirps but shuts the door all the same."

Alliteration

■ "The satisfaction of months shines in his dull pig's eyes as he spits out: 'Dirty hound!'"

■ "What would become of us if everything that happens out there were quite clear to us?"

Euphony

■ "Now red points glow in every face. They comfort me: it looks as though there were little windows in dark village cottages saying that behind them are rooms full of peace."

■ "Outside the window the wind blows and the chestnut trees rustle."

Cacophony

- "But first you have to give the Froggies a good hiding."

- "The storm lashes us, out of the confusion of grey and yellow the hail of splinters whips forth the child-like cries of the wounded, and in the night shattered life groans painfully into silence."

Slang

- "And now get on with it, you old blubber-sticker, and don't you miscount either."

- "You get off scot free, of course."

- "That cooked his goose."

- "Kat has lost all his fun since we have been here, which is bad, for Kat is an old front-hog, and can smell what is coming."

Note: Because this version is the work of translator A. W. Wheen, the creation of images based on English sound—that is, onomatopoeia, alliteration, euphony, cacophony, and slang—cannot be credited to Remarque.

A Note on World War I and Its Technology

Called the "Great War" for its complex involvement of nations extending from northern Europe to northern Africa, western Asia, and the United States, World War I dates officially to Gavrilo Princip's shooting of Austrian Archduke Francis Ferdinand and his wife, Sophie, as they crossed the River Miljachka in Sarajevo, Bosnia, June 28, 1914. Spurred by Serbian terrorism, animosities spread to countries that were interlinked by pacts, treaties, and mutual aims. Late that summer, Germany and Great Britain, trade rivals, and France, which coveted the mineral-rich district of Alsace-Lorraine, entered the fray, which included Czechs, Poles, Romanians, Russians, Bulgarians, Greeks, Arabs, and, eventually, Italians and Turks as well. Germany and Austria-Hungary comprised the Central Powers that invaded Belgium. England, backed by Japan, supported Belgium and declared war on the aggressors. As war fever swept England, fed by hate propaganda on both sides, feisty tommies sang "It's a Long Way to Tipperary" to their girls before leaving for places that many people had never heard of: the Marne and Somme rivers, Jutland, Bruges, Zeebrugge, Verdun, Flanders, Chateau-Thierry, Ypres, Calais, Gallipoli, the Ardennes Forest, and parts of the Falkland Islands.

Unlike wars in past centuries, hapless combatants, armed mainly with bayonet-equipped rifles, faced unforeseen threats, which grew out of expanding mechanization and scientific research:

- **the flamethrower,** a German invention, could hurl a burning stream of gasoline gel at bunkers and pillboxes.

- **chlorine gas** burned the lungs of victims, who either died or lived a miserable invalidism. Against the rules of the Geneva Convention, poisonous gas added a terrifying aspect to an already brutal war. The gas mask, invented by Garrett Augustus Morgan, an African-American, became a regular part of infantry gear.

- **the biplane,** a plane with two sets of wings that could pinpoint troops massing for a ground attack, was enhanced by Anthony Fokker with a **machine gun,** which was synchronized to the turn of the propeller. The plane was frequently involved in dog fights, which Paul and his comrades observe from ground level.

- **high-explosive shells,** frequently mentioned in *All Quiet* as the most tormenting of weapons, augmented by increased accuracy of aim, devastated trench positions and threatened whole towns.

- **the zeppelin,** a hydrogen-filled airship, could glide silently over targets and drop bombs.

- **the U-boat,** a lethal submarine that Germany used to invade British waters and sink supply ships, scuttled the *Lusitania,* a passenger vessel traveling from New York to Liverpool, lost off the coast of Ireland on May 7, 1915, killing 1,196 people.

- **the tank** maneuvered inexorably across all types of terrain—mud, barbed wire, and trenches—on rotating caterpillar treads.

More familiar scourges—hunger, dysentery, typhus, and tetanus—reduced otherwise healthy men to ragged, dispirited wrecks. As war rhetoric continued to push for greater sacrifice, particularly rationing among civilians, many German soldiers, like Detering, grew disillusioned, deserted to defend their families, and were caught, hastily tried, and executed in the field.

The most significant roles in the war effort belonged to Kaiser Wilhelm II, who sought to annex land for Germany, and his top general, Paul von Hindenburg, who faced off against the British commander General Douglas Haig. By April 6, 1917, Germany's aggressive push to bring the United States into the war succeeded. Under President Woodrow Wilson, General John J. "Black Jack" Pershing led two million troops into France, where General Henri Petain headed up local forces. Rapid shifts of loyalties and loss reached a critical point in 1918, after Russia, sunk in its own revolution, deserted the Allied cause. The French reaped their sweetest victory on August 8, with the Second Battle of the Marne, which severely weakened the western front. As fall approached, first Bulgaria, then Turkey and Austria-Hungary surrendered. Germany, crumbling under the weight of severe losses and lack of supplies and reinforcements, capitulated on November 11, a month after the fictional death of Paul Bäumer. Of the more than sixty-four million combatants, eight million died in battle, twenty-one million were injured, and over six and a half million noncombatants were killed.

CliffsNotes Review

Use this CliffsNotes Review to test your understanding of the original text, and reinforce what you've learned in this book. After you work through the review and essay questions, identify the quote section, and the fun and useful practice projects, you're well on your way to understanding a comprehensive and meaningful interpretation *All Quiet on the Western Front*.

Q&A

1. The most dominant subject presented by *All Quiet on the Western Front* is

   a. the effect of World War I on an entire generation.

   b. the causes and mistakes of World War I.

   c. the terrifying nature of trench warfare.

   d. the tremendous gulf between the officers and foot soldiers.

2. The descriptions of nature throughout the book serve this purpose:

   a. to contrast with the horrors of war.

   b. to remind Paul of happier memories.

   c. to show war as unnatural in comparison with nature.

   d. all of the above.

3. As they discuss the nature of war, Paul and his friends cannot understand:

   a. why Germany has not defeated the Allies.

   b. why the Kaiser listens to his subordinates.

   c. why both sides believe their cause is just.

   d. all of the above.

4. Paul's parents and teachers represent:

   a. the Old Germany of patriotic zeal.

   b. the lack of civilian understanding of the war.

   c. the values of the older generation.

   d. all of the above.

5. The title of the novel comes from:

    a. the first line of the peace treaty at the armistice.

    b. the army communique on the day of Paul's death.

    c. the instructions of the Kaiser.

    d. a description from a newspaper headline.

Answers: (1) a. (2) d. (3) c. (4) d. (5) b.

Identify the Quote

1. "There were thousands of Kantoreks, all of whom were convinced that they were acting for the best—in a way that cost them nothing."

2. "It [the rain] falls on our heads and on the heads of the dead up in the line, on the body of the little recruit with the wound that is so much too big for his hip; it falls on Kemmerich's grave; it falls in our hearts."

3. "He fell in October 1918, on a day that was so quiet and still on the whole front, that the army report confined itself to the single sentence: All quiet on the Western Front."

4. "Are you very much afraid?...I would like to tell you to be on your guard against the women out in France. They are no good...And be very careful at the front, Paul...I will pray for you every day, Paul."

5. "Let the months and years come, they can take nothing from me, they can take nothing more. I am so alone, and so without hope that I can confront them without fear."

Answers: (1) Paul is speaking about how teachers and other adults—through the best patriotic beliefs—convinced Paul's generation to enlist and defend the Fatherland. (2) Paul is thinking about the cost of the war, not only in physical wounds, but in wounds to the heart. (3) The author is speaking of the irony of Paul's death on a day just before the Armistice when it is quiet and still. (4) Paul's mother is giving him advice before he goes back to the Front; they can not talk about what matters, only about the details of life. (5) Paul is speaking near the end of his total hopelessness and loss.

Essay Questions

1. Remarque's novel presents nature in many moods and for many purposes. Discuss Remarque's use of nature throughout the novel, using examples when possible.

2. This World War I novel is a story of powerful bonding among men. Using examples from the book, explain how Remarque develops his idea of comradeship in the face of battle.

3. Study the few places where women enter Remarque's novel. What role do they play in his book?

4. From the very title of the novel through the grim ending, Remarque uses irony. Using several examples from the myriad choices, explain his use of irony in the novel.

5. Discuss Remarque's extensive use of simile, particularly in comparing the battlefield with nature.

6. The progress of the war can be seen though the author's descriptions of the few comforts of the front. Paul and his friends are constantly occupied with the search for food, shelter, and the creature comforts. How can the reader follow the progress of the war through their search?

7. Was Paul's death at the end of the novel a blessing or a tragedy? Take a stand and defend your opinion based on the incidents of the novel.

8. Using specific examples from the novel, show how Remarque's descriptions of life at the front seem to reduce humans to animals.

Practice Projects

1. Research war machinery, using some or all of the following: the cluster bomb, flamethrower, machine gun, gas mask, tank, observation balloon, anti-aircraft gun, daisy cutter, star-luster bomb, and grenade. Explain how these devices altered ancient and medieval concepts of the warrior and hero.

2. Compare Paul's response to impending death with that of the speaker in Randall Jarrell's poem "The Death of the Ball Turret Gunner" or Alan Seeger's, "I Have a Rendezvous with Death."

3. Compare Remarque's antiwar sentiments with that of Francis FitzGerald's *Fire in the Lake*, Dee Brown's *Bury My Heart at Wounded Knee* or *Creek*

Mary's Blood, Joseph Heller's *Catch-22*, Walter Dean Myers' *Fallen Angels*, or Dalton Trumbo's *Johnny Got His Gun*.

4. Locate battles at the front from research and make a map showing Paul's company's approximate locations to those battles, using clues from the novel.

5. Create a Web site about the novel, utilizing the author's background, maps, illustrations, themes, and your reaction. Design pages to intrigue and inform your audience, and invite other readers to post their thoughts and responses to their reading of the novel.

6. Compare and contrast this novel with Hemingway's *A Farewell to Arms*, another remarkably realistic early war novel.

7. Create an exhibit of World War I photographs and use quotations from the novel for captions.

8. Use a scene from the novel, such as the one where the men are talking about the nature of war in Chapter Nine, and write dialogue, in the form of a scene from a movie or play; practice and act out the scene with several classmates.

9. Two films of this novel were made, and both are available on videotape. Watch the films and compare the two film versions with the novel.

10. Research information on more recent wars in which technology has rendered killing very distant. How does the soldier's experience in modern warfare compare with what Paul experienced in World War I?

CliffsNotes Resource Center

The learning doesn't need to stop here. CliffsNotes Resource Center shows you the best of the best—links to the best information in print and online about the author and/or related works. And don't think that this is all we've prepared for you; we've put all kinds of pertinent information at www.cliffsnotes.com. Look for all the terrific resources at your favorite bookstore or local library and on the Internet. When you're online, make your first stop www.cliffsnotes.com where you'll find more incredibly useful information about *All Quiet on the Western Front.*

Books

This CliffsNotes book provides a meaningful interpretation of *All Quiet on the Western Front* published by Wiley Publishing, Inc. If you are looking for information about the author and/or related works, check out these other publications:

Erich Maria Remarque, by Christine R. Barker and R. W. Last, uses both English and German research to discuss Remarque's biography and works. New York: Barnes & Noble Books, 1979.

Erich Maria Remarque, A Critical Bio-Bibliography, by C.R. Owen, discusses Remarque's life and includes bibliographies of his work. Amsterdam: Rodopi, 1984.

Erich Maria Remarque: A Literary and Film Biography, by Harley U. Taylor, Jr., discusses the author, his role in German literature, and the film and video adaptations of his novels. New York: Peter Lang, 1989.

Erich Maria Remarque: A Thematic Analysis of His Novels, by Arthur Firda, describes Remarque's novels and gives criticism and interpretation. New York: Peter Lang, 1988.

"Erich Maria Remarque: Shadows in Paradise," by Hans Wagener, in *Exile, the Writer's Experience,* edited by John M. Spalek and Robert F. Bell. Chapel Hill: University of North Carolina Press, 1982. 247–257.

Readings on All Quiet on the Western Front, edited by Terry O'Neill, contains essays about Remarque's novel and includes a bibliography and index. Part of the Greenhaven Press Literary Companion to World Literature. San Diego, California: Greenhaven Press, 1999.

Understanding Erich Maria Remarque, by Hans Wagener, discusses biographical details and interpretation of Remarque's works. Columbia, South Carolina: University of South Carolina Press, 1991.

It's easy to find books published by Wiley Publishing, Inc. You'll find them in your favorite bookstores (on the Internet and at a store near you). We also have three Web sites that you can use to read about all the books we publish:

- ■ www.cliffsnotes.com

- ■ www.dummies.com

- ■ www.wiley.com

Internet

Check out these Web resources for more information about Erich Maria Remarque and *All Quiet on the Western Front*:

All Quiet on the Western Front Information Page, www.bwdd.com/allquiet/ — Information on Remarque; several links to Web sites on World War I and trench warfare; summary of the novel and character sketches.

Erich Maria Remarque Archive, www.lili.uos.de/remarque/internet. htm — Background on the author's life and writings; description of the Remarque Archive founded in 1989 by the city of Osnabruck and the University of Osnabruck; also a description of the Erich Maria Remarque Peace Award.

World War I Web Site, www.geocities.com/SouthBeach/Palms/2460 — Causes of the war; highlights timeline; U-boat information; armistice information; posters from several countries; helpful links to other related Web sites.

World War I: Trenches on the Web, www.worldwar1.com/ — Huge site with history of the war; new material added daily; reference library, maps, theme-based tours, genealogy information, virtual tours, and much more.

The Great War, 1914–1918, www.pitt.edu/~pugachev/greatwar/ww1.html — Huge site with impressive pictures, literary quotations, and a search engine to find relatives who served in World War I; poets and poetry from the war; a slide show of Ypres; many links to other related Web sites.

Next time you're on the Internet, don't forget to drop by www. cliffsnotes.com. We created an online Resource Center that you can use today, tomorrow, and beyond.

Films and Other Recordings

Film and audio versions of novels are often useful as supplements to the book itself. Check out the following two film versions and unabridged audiorecording of *All Quiet on the Western Front*:

All Quiet on the Western Front, Dir. Lewis Milestone. Perf. Lew Ayres and Lewis Wolheim. Universal Pictures, 1930.

All Quiet on the Western Front, Dir. Delbert Mann. Perf. Richard Thomas, Ernest Borgnine, Ian Holm, and Patricia Neal. Marble Arch Productions, 1979.

Remarque, Erich Maria. *All Quiet on the Western Front*. 1928. Read by Simon Calburn. Audiocassette. Chivers Audio Books, 1987.

Check your local library or video store for copies of these versions of Remarque's novel.

Magazines and Journals

The following magazine and journal articles provide additional information on Remarque and *All Quiet on the Western Front*:

Benson, Arnold. "Erich Maria Remarque." *Films in Review* 28 (1994): 28. Discusses Remarque's films and books and how they reveal the sadness and pain of his world. Biography is discussed as well as seven of his books on film.

Chambers, John Whiteclay II. "'All Quiet on the Western Front' (1930): 377. The Antiwar Film and the Image of the First World War." *Historical Journal of Film, Radio and Television* 377 (1994). Discusses relationship of history, the 1930 film, and the war. Describes images from the film that depict the horrors of war.

Richler, Mordecai. "1944: The Year I Learned to Love German." *New York Times Book Review* 1 (1986): 1. Examines the status of the World War I book as a classic study of war.

Check your local library for these articles. You may be able to order them from other libraries if you are not able to find them at your own.

Send Us Your Favorite Tips

In your quest for knowledge, have you ever experienced that sublime moment when you figure out a trick that saves time or trouble? Perhaps you realized you were taking ten steps to accomplish something that could have taken two. Or you found a little-known workaround that achieved great results. If you've discovered a useful tip that helped you study more effectively and you'd like to share it, the CliffsNotes staff would love to hear from you. Go to our Web site at www.cliffsnotes.com and click the Talk to Us button. If we select your tip, we may publish it as part of CliffsNotes Daily, our exciting, free e-mail newsletter. To find out more or to subscribe to a newsletter, go to on the Web.

Index

CliffsNotes

LITERATURE NOTES

Absalom, Absalom!
The Aeneid
Agamemnon
Alice in Wonderland
All the King's Men
All the Pretty Horses
All Quiet on the
    Western Front
All's Well &
    Merry Wives
American Poets of the
    20th Century
American Tragedy
Animal Farm
Anna Karenina
Anthem
Antony and Cleopatra
Aristotle's Ethics
As I Lay Dying
The Assistant
As You Like It
Atlas Shrugged
Autobiography of
    Ben Franklin
Autobiography of
    Malcolm X
The Awakening
Babbit
Bartleby & Benito
    Cereno
The Bean Trees
The Bear
The Bell Jar
Beloved
Beowulf
The Bible
Billy Budd & Typee
Black Boy
Black Like Me
Bleak House
Bless Me, Ultima
The Bluest Eye & Sula
Brave New World
Brothers Karamazov

The Call of the Wild &
    White Fang
Candide
The Canterbury Tales
Catch-22
Catcher in the Rye
The Chosen
The Color Purple
Comedy of Errors…
Connecticut Yankee
The Contender
The Count of
    Monte Cristo
Crime and Punishment
The Crucible
Cry, the Beloved
    Country
Cyrano de Bergerac
Daisy Miller &
    Turn…Screw
David Copperfield
Death of a Salesman
The Deerslayer
Diary of Anne Frank
Divine Comedy-I.
    Inferno
Divine Comedy-II.
    Purgatorio
Divine Comedy-III.
    Paradiso
Doctor Faustus
Dr. Jekyll and Mr. Hyde
Don Juan
Don Quixote
Dracula
Electra & Medea
Emerson's Essays
Emily Dickinson Poems
Emma
Ethan Frome
The Faerie Queene
Fahrenheit 451
Far from the Madding
    Crowd
A Farewell to Arms
Farewell to Manzanar
Fathers and Sons
Faulkner's Short Stories

Faust Pt. I & Pt. II
The Federalist
Flowers for Algernon
For Whom the Bell Tolls
The Fountainhead
Frankenstein
The French
    Lieutenant's Woman
The Giver
Glass Menagerie &
    Streetcar
Go Down, Moses
The Good Earth
The Grapes of Wrath
Great Expectations
The Great Gatsby
Greek Classics
Gulliver's Travels
Hamlet
The Handmaid's Tale
Hard Times
Heart of Darkness &
    Secret Sharer
Hemingway's
    Short Stories
Henry IV Part 1
Henry IV Part 2
Henry V
House Made of Dawn
The House of the
    Seven Gables
Huckleberry Finn
I Know Why the
    Caged Bird Sings
Ibsen's Plays I
Ibsen's Plays II
The Idiot
Idylls of the King
The Iliad
Incidents in the Life of
    a Slave Girl
Inherit the Wind
Invisible Man
Ivanhoe
Jane Eyre
Joseph Andrews
The Joy Luck Club
Jude the Obscure

Julius Caesar
The Jungle
Kafka's Short Stories
Keats & Shelley
The Killer Angels
King Lear
The Kitchen God's Wife
The Last of the
    Mohicans
Le Morte d'Arthur
Leaves of Grass
Les Miserables
A Lesson Before Dying
Light in August
The Light in the Forest
Lord Jim
Lord of the Flies
The Lord of the Rings
Lost Horizon
Lysistrata & Other
    Comedies
Macbeth
Madame Bovary
Main Street
The Mayor of
    Casterbridge
Measure for Measure
The Merchant
    of Venice
Middlemarch
A Midsummer Night's
    Dream
The Mill on the Floss
Moby-Dick
Moll Flanders
Mrs. Dalloway
Much Ado About
    Nothing
My Ántonia
Mythology
Narr. …Frederick
    Douglass
Native Son
New Testament
Night
1984
Notes from the
    Underground

Check Out the All-New CliffsNotes Guides

TECHNOLOGY TOPICS

PERSONAL FINANCE TOPICS

CAREER TOPICS